D0389538

Peasant Wisdom

Peasant Wisdom

Cultural Adaptation
in a Swiss Village

Daniela Weinberg

UNIVERSITY OF CALIFORNIA PRESS

BERKELEY · LOS ANGELES · LONDON

University of California press
Berkeley and Los Angeles, California

University of California Press, Ltd.
London, England

Copyright © 1975, by
The Regents of the University of California

ISBN 0-520-02789-2
Library of Congress Catalog Card Number: 74-79776
Printed in the United States of America

301.352
W 423p

194053

To J, who waited

JUST LET THEM COME AND SEE HOW GOOD IT IS HERE—BET-
TER THAN IN THEIR OFFICES, THEIR PRISONS, THEIR
STREETS. BUT THEY COULD NOT COME EVEN IF THEY
WANTED TO. IT'S TOO HIGH AND STEEP FOR THEM, THOSE
JUDGES; TOO OLD, THOSE GOVERNMENT GENTLEMEN KNOT-
TED WITH RHEUMATISM; TOO WELL FED, THOSE POLICE
OFFICERS. THE MOUNTAINS, FREEDOM . . .

FARINET

Contents

Preface

THE QUICKENING PACE OF CHANGE THROWS INTO RELIEF
MECHANISMS OF FUNCTIONING AND CHANGE THAT ARE
USUALLY OBLITERATED BY THEIR SLOWNESS AND THE WAY
IN WHICH THEY OVERLAP WITHIN THE GENERAL TRANSITION.
(MENDRAS 1970:15)

Anthropologists trying to understand complex societies have
tended to focus on small, relatively isolated communities—a
path well trodden and clearly marked by earlier students of
primitive cultures. Though this book does focus on a small
and relatively isolated Swiss Alpine village, Bruson is not
considered as a bounded unit but as an adaptive system interacting with a real environment. From its early origins, through
its remembered past, and to its present day, Bruson's "world"
has challenged the persistence of its culture. To document the
history of Bruson is to be impressed by the continuity of social
structure and belief system—in spite of obvious changes in the
economy.

The community-study method, while rich in detail and
insight, is self-limiting. By modeling a community as discrete,
distinctive, and closed, it forces us to model change as a series
of step functions responding directly to variables "outside" the
system. A logical consequence is to imagine a threshold of
change beyond which a new culture emerges. Such a model

obliterates subtle distinctions in the nature of culture change—especially the important difference between regulation and adaptation. Since environment is never static, a culture is incessantly making regulatory responses—some of which catch the eye as "changes." Only when the regulatory process breaks down is *true* change—adaptation—observed. And only then can we properly and usefully speak of a new culture.

The people of Bruson, living in a modern capitalist state and served by the conveniences of industrial development, continue to act as if they were subsistence farmers free of entangling alliances beyond their small world of village and commune. This behavior is evident in their relations with kin, with other villagers, and with the outside world. Supporting these social relations is an ideology of "peasant wisdom" that goes far back in time—to the autonomous Alpine republics of the Middle Ages—and is maintained in the contemporary federalist nation-state of Switzerland. In Bruson, the evolutionary process has taken the form of successive regulation rather than precipitous adaptation. For this reason, it is more meaningful to study culture change by focusing on what has remained the same.

This study is based on field research conducted in Bruson between December 1967 and September 1969. The actual field research was preceded, in the spring of 1967, by three months of preliminary survey in the Valais. During the fieldwork period that followed, I was a full-time resident of the village for a total of nineteen months—sixteen between December 1967 and March 1969, and the remaining three during the summer of 1969. My research method was essentially that of participant observation, including a wide range of activities from formal interviewing to functioning as accompanist for the village singing society.

This work is written in the "ethnographic present"—that period of time which I observed directly while in the field. Besides the expected demographic fluctuations in the size and composition of the population, the only important change since that time is the political enfranchisement of women at the cantonal (1970) and federal (1971) levels. I have incorporated this change in the work, but only through mechanical revision of the text. The cultural implications of women's suffrage remain to be studied.

During the first five months of fieldwork, I lived in the apartment occupied by Clara and Félix Besse and owned by Ida Vaudan. Later I lived in the house of Marguerite and Jean Fellay, and, for the last three months, in the chalet of Louise Gard. During the entire period, I took most of my meals at the Café Chez Rosy, belonging to the Maret-Deslarzes family. All these people I gratefully acknowledge for the patience, kindness, and understanding which they extended to a stranger among them.

I wish to express thanks to Eric R. Wolf, Chairman of my doctoral committee, who helped me always precisely at the right time and precisely in the right way. I also acknowledge with gratitude the other members of my committee for their invaluable assistance in helping me to clarify my thoughts: Horace M. Miner, Anatol Rapoport, and Mischa Titiev. The research was supported in part by a Ford Foundation Grant, administered by the University of Michigan Department of Anthropology.

Grateful acknowledgment is also due to the IBM European Systems Research Institute in Geneva for the use of their IBM System 360/Model 50—specifically to Dr. Carlo Santacroce, first Director of the Institute, Georges Psarofaghis, Administrative Manager, and René Vaucher, Librarian.

I wish to extend thanks also to the many people who helped me find my way in the relatively uncharted territory of Swiss ethnological research: Raoul Naroll, Isac Chiva, and André Benguerel, who initially put me in touch with European peasantry specialists and with Brusonins; the Swiss scholars Georges Amoudruz, the late Pierre Conne, André Donnet, Max Gschwend, Georges Lobsiger, Georges Nicolas, Marc Sauter, Rose Claire Schüle, Erich Schwabe, Karl Suter, and Jean Vallat; and earlier researchers in Bagnes, Odile Andan and Elizabeth Gossop Williams.

I acknowledge with gratitude the two Presidents of the Commune of Bagnes during the period of my fieldwork, Théophile Fellay and Willy Ferrez, as well as *M. le curé* Louis

Ducrey and *M. le curé* Alexis Rouiller, Francis Perraudin, teacher at the Collège and unofficial historian of the valley, and Marthe Carron, officer of the *Etat Civil*.

I am especially indebted to my students whose critical curiosity about peasants encouraged me, and particularly to those who shared with me their field materials and insights: Ziporah Elstein and Douglas Barden (Hérémence), Nancy Mittleman (Cravegna), Sonia Rosenberg (St.-Colomban-des-Villards) and Roberta Zucker (Trient). In addition, I wish to thank those colleagues who have made available to me their field notes and other unpublished materials: Robert K. Burns, Jr. (St.-Véran), John Friedl (Kippel), Robert McC. Netting (Törbel), and Randy Reiter and Rayna R. Reiter (Colpied).

To my husband, Gerald M. Weinberg, I owe thanks for his professional services as computer programmer but, far more important, for not only tolerating but actually enjoying the entire undertaking. Gratitude is also due my sister-in-law, Cheryl Plum, who typed the original manuscript with devotion and intelligence, and Mary Lou Kepler, who assisted immeasurably in the final stages.

The greatest debt of all I owe to the people of Bruson, who taught me so much.

... these I will write of are human beings, living in this world, innocent of such twistings as these which are taking place over their heads ... they were dwelt among, investigated, spied on, revered, and loved, by other quite monstrously alien human beings ... they are now being looked into by still others, who have picked up their living as casually as if it were a book. (James Agee, *Let Us Now Praise Famous Men*)

Part I

The Background

1. Some Theoretical Issues

A frequent and urgent theme in European studies is the *exode rural*—the abandonment of rural areas—and the new relationships between city and country that have grown out of a century of industrialization. On the one hand, this exodus of rural peoples threatens the primary economic sector of agriculture; on the other hand, it seriously disrupts the lifeways of a large proportion of the world's population. Sons of agriculturalists are attracted by the lures of city life and wage labor—material goods and less arduous working conditions. At the same time, traditional forms of agriculture are being undermined or eliminated by the more profitable mechanization of large-scale farming, In all parts of the world, small-scale, familistic, labor-intensive farming has become a marginal occupation, and the peasant a marginal man in the socio-economic structure.

In Switzerland this problem is highlighted and made more acute by the nature of the geography: two-thirds of the land area of the nation is mountainous, and less than 30 percent of this mountainous land can be considered arable. Nevertheless, about three-quarters of all Swiss agriculturalists live in the mountain regions. While the proportion of the Swiss population practicing agriculture has diminished from 37 percent in 1888 to 10 percent in 1963 (Gabert and Guichonnet 1965:194),

3

most of this diminution has taken place in the non-mountainous regions which have become industrialized and where mechanization has supplanted traditional farming techniques. In the Valais, for instance—a mountain canton with an average altitude of 2,290 meters and one of the major agricultural regions in Switzerland—55 percent of the active population in the high valleys (above 800 meters) is still engaged in agriculture (Loup 1965:185).

A great portion of this agricultural enterprise—in the Valais and in the nation as a whole—is subsidized by the federal and cantonal governments. Aid is offered particularly to mountain agriculturalists, in spite of the fact that mountain agriculture is the most difficult and the least profitable in terms of labor requirements. The reasons for this support are intimately tied to the national policy of political neutrality, which depends on economic self-sufficiency and military self-defense. Every effort has been made, therefore, to combat the exode rural, including subsidization of both individuals and economic cooperatives to encourage crop diversification, modernization of equipment, experimentation; strong tariff protection of Swiss agricultural produce; subsistence and educational support for mountain families and the aged; and, finally, the propagation of an ideology which extols the traditional values of rural life.

> Thus, there is official celebration of the physical and moral qualities of mountain populations. They possess the basic virtues: they are blessed with good health; they are adapted to the mountains with which they are perfectly acquainted from their long and difficult walks over a variegated terrain; they present great resistance to poor weather and fatigue; they are a very sober people. Their religious faith imposes a very strict individual and social morality: Valaisans are scrupulously honest; their morals are austere; village solidarity, essential to the hard conditions of life, is the rule. The mountains are a kind of preserve for the national morality. (Loup 1965: 119-120)

The economic problem of exode rural, thus, impinges directly upon the question of national politics and ideology. The political policy of neutrality is the direct result of the historical development of Swiss federalism. The Confederation of "states"

—the cantons—grew in response to military and political pressures from European neighbors. The essential purpose of the Confederation was and still is to preserve the autonomy of its member states—that is, to preserve and protect their differences rather than to homogenize and suppress these differences. This principle of unity through diversity, together with an active policy of neutrality which has put Switzerland in the role of arbiter in international affairs, is an inspiration to modern proponents of European federalism. Swiss federalism has produced a *"démocratie-témoin"* (Siegfried 1948), a model democracy, and a *"peuple heureux,"* a happy nation.

> The word "happy" . . . simply means that the country is at peace, that it is prosperous, and, above all, that its political and social regime is approved by an immense majority of the citizens while the minority opposition complains mostly of being a minority! . . . More than a nation, beautiful as it is, and more than a people, as "happy" as I have said, the name of Switzerland signifies a certain form of community existence, a certain structure of public relationships, the supremely paradoxical idea, if one reflects on it, of a *society of free men.* (Rougemont 1965:7, 13.)

In dealing with ideological foundations, or "world view," in a complex culture, one is inevitably concerned with Robert Redfield's model of "Great" and "Little" Traditions (Redfield 1956). The model postulates a distinction between the "high culture" of the urban elite—expressed especially in the intellectual and artistic production of what Redfield called the "reflective few"—and the local folkways of the "unreflective many." The peasantry—bearers of the Little Tradition—underwrite the Great Tradition elite through their surplus agricultural production. Both Traditions together make up Redfield's conception of "civilization."

In Swiss culture, it would seem, the Great Tradition of political neutrality is supported by the Little Tradition of participatory democracy in a "society of free men." The Great Tradition, which produces "a happy people"—prosperous, urban, and industrialized—depends on the Little Tradition lived daily by the agricultural mountain peasant. Following this line of reasoning, however, quickly drives one into the misty realm of anthropological mythology. While the analytic device of Great and Little Traditions may be useful in studying other cultures, it only obscures the facts of Swiss culture.

In Swiss cosmology, there is no sharp dichotomy between city and country insofar as personal contacts are concerned. Every autonomous state in the Confederation—that is, every canton—contains both rural and urban areas which are mutually interdependent. Because of the decentralization of the political organization, both at national and cantonal levels, no urban center dominates, in the way that Paris dominates the French nation or London the British. When a Valaisan speaks of "the capital," he is referring neither to Sion, the cantonal capital, nor to Bern, the federal capital, but to Paris.

There is a great deal of exchange of personnel between rural and urban areas, and most Swiss city-dwellers seem to have family roots, as well as contemporary relatives, in the mountains. City-dwellers and their country cousins agree on the superiority of the climate—both natural and social—of the mountains. The mountain residents are also the first to describe contemptuously the poor medical and commercial facilities available to them locally and their consequent need for the city. While city-dwellers go to the mountains for recreational purposes, mountain people have traditionally turned to the cities for better employment opportunities.

Although it is undoubtedly true that rural children lack certain educational and career possibilities which are more readily available to urban children, the Swiss system of occupational training acts as a countervailing force. Because every occupation is raised to the status of a *métier*, or trade, with its prescribed number of years of training and a graduated system of certificates of proficiency, no occupation inherently lacks dignity. Education is highly valued, and there is universal literacy based on cantonal requirements for compulsory education to the age of sixteen for rural and urban children alike.

The Swiss peasant enjoys an unusually high standard of living. His image of the good life is based on the cultural stability and continuity of his community and on his personal independence within that community, expressed in ownership of his house and lands. Far from being an innocent rustic, easily manipulable by unprincipled and self-interested urban politicians, he is a formidable and sophisticated participant in Swiss democracy—and, more often than not, a distant cousin of the city politician.

Having painted this picture of the Swiss peasant and his urban compatriots, it becomes difficult to accept the analytic relevance and utility of Great and Little Traditions. It is tempting to say that, in Switzerland, there is only one tradition with a variety of visible manifestations. It is, perhaps, for this reason, that cultural-anthropological studies of Swiss communities are few.

The holistic anthropological study of one's own culture is a relatively recent phenomenon. European anthropology has traditionally distinguished between studies of "folklore"—that is, studies of one's own cultural heritage—and ethnological studies—studies of other cultures. This distinction really expresses the ethnocentric view that one's own culture is not a Culture—a view that will be familiar to all anthropological fieldworkers who have been frustrated by a feeling that their subjects were concealing information, when actually they were simply not aware of possessing anthropological data.

Folklore studies are atomistic and antiquarian. They are based on the acceptance of the Great and Little Tradition dichotomy. Just as this seems a rather bizarre and meaningless dichotomy in the Swiss context, so too Swiss folklorists are regarded as eccentric people. My peasant informants, in fact, often used the term "folklore" in a nostalgic or denigrating manner to indicate something which was old-fashioned or insignificant. I was told that, to understand the village and "*sortir quelque chose de valable*" (to produce something worthwhile), I needed to understand only three things: the *laiterie* (a cooperative dairy), the fruit and vegetable syndicate (a cooperative devoted to chemical spraying and to marketing of cash crops), and the recently initiated tourist development of the village.

While this advice betrays an ethnocentric blindness to one's own culture, dismissing as "folklore" everything except recently introduced and non-traditional institutions, it also suggests that one suspend theoretical judgment until the facts of the case have been considered.

Bruson is a village of 250 people in the Commune of Bagnes,

Canton of Valais. Its traditional economic base is a mixture
of agriculture and pastoralism, which has been supplemented
in recent times by the introduction of new market crops,
opportunities for wage labor in the valley, and, most recently,
an indigenous attempt to create a small ski resort.

Although the population has followed general rural trends
in the last half-century by decreasing some 40 percent, Brusonins believe that this decline has now ceased, and, in fact, they
prefer to speak of an *exode agricole* rather than an exode rural.
Very few today live solely from agriculture, but the degree of
dependence on the land is partially concealed by the method
of calculating income in strictly monetary terms. In actual fact,
even the part-time agriculturalist owes a large portion of his
livelihood to his farming activities, which provide both food
staples and rent-free housing for his family.

The idea of an exode agricole does not express an absolute
abandonment of agriculture but rather a change of emphasis
in the economic structure. Today it is agriculture that is
considered the supplementary method of producing income. To
the extent that there is an exode agricole, it is only partial
and temporary. While the young men seek training in métiers,
claiming that there is neither money nor future in mountain
agriculture, they do, in fact, return to the land after marriage
and practice at least a limited subsistence agriculture. The
reasons for this are simple and clear: the land is there—the
couple's present or promised inheritance; with the acquisition
of a wife and, eventually, children, a man has an adequate
and cost-free labor force to practice an *agriculture accessoire*
(supplementary agriculture) sufficient for household needs and
some extra cash.

This shift in emphasis has been accompanied by an improvement in agricultural conditions. In the past forty years, cantonal subsidies to mountain agriculturalists have contributed, in
Bruson, to the establishment of several economic cooperatives
as well as to necessary amelioration of the *alpages*, the high
summer pastures. These improvements, by calling into play
communal organizations, have removed a large part of the
agricultural burden from the individual, thus making feasible
his continuance as an agriculturalist. Government agricultural
services have also encouraged diversification of land use, and

Brusonins have responded, in part, by turning to tourism. The hope is that the ski development, while temporally extending the use of the Bruson territory, will also provide local employment and an alternative to emigration.

The Brusonin's economic dependence on governmental aid is balanced by the political autonomy of his native community. This autonomy is attributable to the national system of federalism, which is said to have had its origin in 1291 in the famous pact of the Forest Cantons (now the cantons of Uri, Schwyz, Obwald, and Unterwald). These four communities, originally called *Waldstätten*, were "cooperatives or communes of the forest, associations of the people of a valley who own the land corporately" (Rougemont 1965:34).

The commune has historical primacy and contemporary political supremacy. It is the most homogeneous unit in the Swiss political system: its corporately-owned territory is usually bounded by natural geographic features, and its people are linked by strong commonality of language, religion, history, occupation, and special interests related to all these. The commune is an autonomous administrative unit with a population composed of *bourgeois*, or native members, and other residents. To be a Swiss citizen means to be a bourgeois (or naturalized bourgeois) of one of approximately 3,000 communes.

The canton, or "state" in modern usage, is a larger and more impersonal administrative unit which participates directly in the Confederation. While a *confédéré* (citizen of the Confederation) must be a bourgeois of a commune, the basic articles of confederation permit complete freedom of movement for any confédéré within the nation. Statistics on this movement provide a measure of the relative cultural stability of various parts of Switzerland. The nation as a whole has shown a drastic change in configuration since 1850, the year of the first federal census. At that time, 64 percent of the population lived in their native communes and another 26 percent in other communes of the native canton. In 1960, only 25 percent of the Swiss population resided in their native communes and another 30 percent in the native canton.

Today, the mountain agricultural regions have the highest proportion of residents who are natives of that canton. In the

Valais, for instance, 85 percent of the residents are native to
the canton. In Bruson, just over 90 percent of all registered
voters (men over twenty) are bourgeois of Bagnes. Of the
forty-three children of resident Brusonins who have married
and no longer live in the natal household, 50 percent still live
in the commune (half of these in Bruson or its tiny dependent
hamlet of Le Sappey), and another 30 percent live in other
parts of the Valais. The political autonomy of the commune
is thus supported by a largely indigenous population.

At the commune level of organization, the Brusonin's community is a well-defined unit with a high degree of cultural
homogeneity. The Commune of Bagnes—with a population of
about 4,800—coincides with the geographic valley; the commune was, until very recently, a single parish—until the village
of Verbier grew into an enormous resort and established its own
church. As a political and economic unit, the commune is
self-governing and self-taxing, and it provides various administrative and welfare services to its population; the native language of all Bagnards is a patois peculiar to the valley and
showing some variation from one village to another; finally,
the commune acts as a unit with respect to certain special
economic and social problems—the sharing of profits derived
from the great hydroelectric plant at the end of the valley,
and the attempts to exploit and control the rapid economic
ascension of Verbier.

The relationship between the Confederation and the communes is reproduced in microcosm by that between the commune and its villages. The commune is grouped with other
communes (through the canton structure) to form the maximal
administrative unit, the Confederation. The village, although
not autonomous, has cultural integrity within the larger administrative unit of the commune. Bruson is one of a dozen
major villages in Bagnes. Like the other villages, Bruson is
politically dependent on the commune, having no formal government of its own. This dependence has grown—generally to
the advantage of the villages—as physical communication has
increased within the valley during the last half-century. The
villages have, however, retained their unique cultural identities
—that is, their right to be different. In this way, federalism
permeates the entire national system, down to the smallest

components of commune and village. In paraphrase of Rouge-mont's description of the Confederation, one may say that the Swiss commune embodies the paradox of a "society of free villages."

Having described Bruson as a modified but still agricultural village with certain dependent relations with the larger polity of commune and Confederation, we can now consider the question of its cultural integrity and stability. The local trans-lation of exode rural into exode agricole and the actual imple-mentation of this principle give evidence of economic stability. Swiss federalism and its replication at the commune level, along with the absence of polarized Great and Little Traditions, provide a context for political identity.

To hypothesize that these economic and political features contribute to the cultural integrity of Bruson, one must discov-er the supporting social and ideological structures. I shall follow the analogy of Swiss federalism and its formula of "unity through diversity." This model requires the identification and description of the separate social units involved—the household and various higher-level structures within the village—and of the ideology which holds them together.

2. The Village

Bruson is situated at 1,050 meters on one of several terraces on the south slope of the valley. (See Maps 1 and 2.) This exposition means that the village receives relatively little sun and has a shortened growing season, but the terrace location makes agriculture possible to a greater extent than in other villages on the steep valley slopes. The winter situation is similarly one of mixed blessings: fewer daylight hours and less sun make the region less attractive to skiers, but these same features guarantee better and longer-lasting snow, while the presence of forests prevents avalanches.

Bruson, like most of the central region of the Valais, has a climate characterized by sharp seasonal contrast of temperature and precipitation and a low overall precipitation for the year. The commune seat of Bagnes, Le Châble, at 830 meters, has an average annual precipitation of about 30 inches—most of this falling as snow in the winter, and the driest months being June through August. In Bruson, the extremes of temperature are about -5° F. in winter and about 90° F. in summer. This is one of the few regions in southern Switzerland which receives the Foehn—a southerly wind which dramatically raises the temperature, melts snows, and lowers relative humidity. Many writers impressionistically describe this climate as "Mediterranean," because of its winds, its hot dry summers, and its frequently sunny skies.

Map 1. Switzerland.

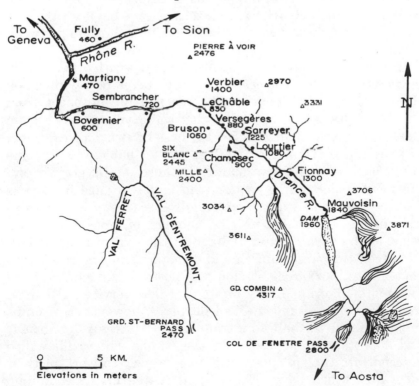

Map 2. The Valley of Bagnes.

Le Châble has been connected to the outside by railroad since about 1950, at which time the other villages in the valley were served by postal bus. A paved road, completed about 1954, connects Bruson with Le Châble, three kilometers below in the river basin. About one kilometer down this road from Bruson is the hamlet of Le Sappey with its sixty-six inhabitants living in fifteen households. About half of the Sappajous, as they are called, are related to Brusonins, and the hamlet has traditionally been divided in various functions between dependence on Bruson and on Le Châble. Although most Sappajous still bring their milk to Le Châble for processing, more and more send their children to the recently-built Bruson primary school, engage with Brusonins in cooperative marketing of their cash crops, and participate in the Bruson-based sections of the valley's two major political parties. A small chapel was recently dedicated in Le Sappey, but the hamlet has no other public facilities such as stores or cafés. Consequently, the presence of Sappajous in Bruson is common, and, with long-standing patterns of intermarriage between the two communities, there has also been much migration between them.

Brusonins also have kinship and affinal ties with other nearby villages—especially Versegères and Prarreyer below them on the slope, both of which can be reached by footpaths from Bruson. Other social contacts with these villages arise from the contiguity of their *alpages* to those of Bruson. A number of Brusonins have married natives of Le Châble and, in some cases, have moved there—mainly because of the greater employment opportunities in this, the largest village in Bagnes and the most important commercially because of its access to the outside. Le Châble may be thought of, on a very small scale, as the urban center of Bagnes: the seat of government, the site of the parish church and cemetery, the transportation center with its railroad station and postal bus depot, and the location of shops and very limited medical services. For most major commercial and medical purposes, however, Brusonins prefer to make the half-hour train trip to Martigny, an ancient and important urban center in the Rhône valley. They also descend into the valley several times a year to work in their vineyards, which have always been located in the commune of Fully on the right bank of the Rhône.

Little is known about the early history and settlement of Bagnes. Some Bronze Age and Roman Era remains—artifacts and burials—have been found, especially in the villages such as Bruson and Verbier high up on both slopes. It is probably this evidence, meager and poorly described as it is, that leads Bagnards to believe that these high villages were settled first and that there used to be a deep lake where the river and the low villages now exist.

The first written records relating to the valley date from the twelfth century when control of Bagnes was transferred from the House of Savoy to the Abbot of St. Maurice. Brusonin family names first appear in the valley records in the thirteenth century. In fact, surnames were very uncommon in the region until about the fourteenth century, and it is difficult to find written evidence of the existence of the village until the middle of the seventeenth century when the present chapel was built. In the fourteenth century, silver mines above Bruson were first exploited. For four hundred years they provided fuel for political competition in the Valais, until they were finally abandoned in 1723 when the silver was depleted.

Brusonins have no concept of and little interest in the time depth of their village. They are aware of the archaeological finds in the region and sometimes speak of history in relation to place-names—but seldom agree on their interpretations. For instance, the region called Changemaux, at the eastern end of Bruson territory, is variously explained etymologically as *champ des morts* (cemetery) or *changes des maux* (evil-inspired changes)—the latter referring to a tale of sorcerers alleged to have lived there. A more probable interpretation, tracing the word through its original patois form, suggests that the region was a stopping place for cows on their way to the alpage—hence, a sort of *mayen*, or intermediate pasture.

Brusonins are aware of a potential archaeological site that is not mentioned in the literature—a small area, about ten minutes' walk from the village, where several regular depressions are evident. This region is called Biollay-les-Raccards—Biollay of the Barns—on the assumption that barns or perhaps even dwellings once stood in these depressions, forming a kind of hamlet. A story is told about female witches who lived in this hamlet and were responsible for the disappearance of village youths who wandered out there. No one living today recalls ever having seen structures on the spot, so it is difficult to determine the age of the presumed hamlet.

There are other named locations outside the village in its immediate surroundings of cultivated fields (*champs*) and hay-fields (*prés*), the more distant mayens which reach an altitude of 1,600 meters, and the highest summer pastures (*alpages*) rising to 2,600 meters. The village itself is divided into ten or twelve named *quartiers* (neighborhoods), most of whose names are used regularly and the boundaries of which are generally known.

The three "major" quartiers are located at the angles of the roughly triangular shape of the village. The names of two of these refer specifically to that shape—Le Fond (the bottom) and Le Sommet (the top)—and the third, Le Clou, is a place-name for the region just outside the village which touches on the quartier. Other quartier names refer, in similar fashion, to locations on the triangle (La Cotze, the patois word for corner), to the traditional name of a contiguous field, or to some feature of the quartier—La Fontaine (the fountain), Vers la Chapelle (near the chapel), Crête à Dzera (the patois for "Gerald's crest," referring to the steep road ascending into this quartier).

All but the three "major" quartiers are considered *sous-quartiers* (sub-neighborhoods), being smaller and, in some cases, consisting only of a single dwelling. In recent expansion of the village, new residential quartiers have been established in what were previously contiguous fields; they take their names from the existing place-names. Finally, a nickname is applied to a no-longer-existing quartier (or, perhaps, to one that still exists but has changed in name and character—there is variation of opinion on this point). The existence of the "Quartier des Juifs" (Jewish quarter) came to my attention only by accident, and most informants who spoke of it did so with a mixture of amusement and embarrassment. The name refers to a group of past residents—the quartier now is largely abandoned, in-habited chiefly by a few old people—who were evidently wealth-ier than other villagers and, on this basis, were caricatured as being *plus adroits* (more shrewd) with money and identified contemptuously as *commerçants* (merchants).

The slope of the village land is, at some points, as great as

30°, and the buildings are laid out in rows that traverse the slope. While most dwellings are interspersed with agricultural outbuildings, these outbuildings dominate in some parts of the village. The two- or three-story dwellings, made of stone and often faced with masonry, are easily distinguished from the dark wooden outbuildings. The total effect of the village, seen from above or below, is characteristic of Valaisan villages—a small, huddled, undifferentiated knot of structures. This external impresssion stands in sharp contrast to the high degree of native differentiation evidenced by the great number of quartiers in this small area, and by the varied character and functions of these quartiers.

In earlier times, the social and economic structure of the village was expressed through the quartiers, which represented separate socio-economic units based on internal mutual aid. Each quartier maintained its communal bread-baking oven and its fountain, supplying washing and drinking water to the quartier residents. Today villagers buy bread at the store, and the commune has taken over responsibility for providing water. Every dwelling but one has water piped to it, and the fountains are now used only for preliminary washing of stable boots or large quantities of produce. Residents of the quartier, in the past, were also responsible for each other's social welfare. When a resident died, his quartier neighbors took charge of the funeral and acted as *porteurs* (pall-bearers). Today this general function has passed to the village as a whole, while porteurs are usually selected from among the neighbors or co-workers of the deceased—whether or not they reside in the village.

What remains of these socio-economic units today is a feeling that each quartier has a special character, based either on the personality of its residents—thus, one quartier is described as being more friendly and less given to internal squabbling than another—or on some feature of special interest located in the quartier—the chapel, a café, a store. With the exception of the new school, which stands just below the village, public buildings are in the village itself and scattered among the various quartiers: two cafés (in Le Clou and Le Fond), the chapel, the old school which is now used as a youth hostel (in the Chapelle quartier), the *laiterie* (at the edge of the village in a quartier called Les Gilles), two *épiceries*, or general stores (in Crête à Dzera and La Fontaine), and a recently-constructed *pension* (just outside the village in an area called Les Grands Vergers—the great orchards).

The cafés and the laiterie are important social centers, essentially exclusive to men, while the épiceries are visited with more or less equal frequency by men, women, and children. Cafés as public and commercial drinking places are a fairly recent phenomenon in Bruson. Men used to do their drinking either in their *caves* (wine cellars) or in their family kitchens. Apparently, certain men became known either for their hospitality or for the quality and quantity of their wine, and certain kitchens or caves were more frequented than others—becoming, in effect, semi-public drinking centers, visited mainly on weekends since little cash was available for daily drinking. The modern café as a commercial enterprise, operating on a regular daily schedule, first appeared about forty-five years ago and grew in popularity as more money became available and as fewer men were growing more wine-grapes than those required for household consumption. The development of the modern café is reflected in the frequently heard description of it as "the poor man's cave."

The cave, in modern Bruson, is an essential feature of every dwelling and remains, to a limited extent, the place where a man entertains his friends. The kitchen, too, has retained some of its earlier function as the central and most important room. Most households today occupy one apartment (one floor) of a house. An oil-heating system has been installed in most apartments—usually a space heater but sometimes central heating—but the kitchen, with its wood-burning *potager* (stove), remains the center of activity. The potager used to be the only kitchen equipment, used both for heating and for cooking. Today, however, most kitchens are also equipped with an electric range and stove—electricity being abundant because of the hydroelectric plant at the end of the valley—and the potager is used only for long-cooking items such as large quantities of potatoes (a traditional food staple) and the traditional *lessive* (laundry) pot for boiling laundry.

Following the kitchen in importance, in earlier times, was the parents' bedroom—the only other heated place in the apartments—usually a space heater but sometimes central potstone, known for its excellent heat-retaining properties. This *fourneau aux pierres ollaires*, usually engraved with the builder's initials and the date of construction, has become a sought-after item by antique collectors. Many Brusonins deeply regret having sold their fourneaux; others are proud to have retained theirs and have converted them to oil use.

Although Brusonins show little curiosity about the early history of their village, they exhibit great pride in persisting traditions and surviving objects of the past. Several villagers proudly claim to live in the oldest house in the village. When asked for its precise age, however, they reveal ignorance and also a certain casual disinterest. One hundred years is considered "old" for a house, when actually, the oldest house in the village is clearly marked as having been built in 1782.

When I asked a number of informants which was, in their opinion, the most beautiful house in the village, one answered that it was his own—in a humorous spirit but with evident sincerity of belief. Although most families own only the apartment they occupy in a house, this ownership is another source of pride—as well as a problem. As a result of the rapid population decline in this century, a number of houses or parts of houses have not been occupied for many years. They are considered unlivable by modern standards, although newly-married couples have great difficulty finding housing in the village. Three young couples in the village today rent apartments, even though their families own extra housing space. Since this space requires much improvement to bring it up to modern standards, these couples prefer to rent with the hope of eventually building a new house on family lands. But even rental units of "livable" quality are hard to find or else too expensive for a Brusonin—having been recently modernized with an eye to tourist rental. What housing is available, therefore, is unacceptable—either because of its low quality or because of its high quality. The only alternative, then, is to move out of the village. In this way, population decline, combined with the elevation of housing standards, has had two major effects: the residential expansion of the village into previously agricultural regions, and the stimulation of further population decline through forced emigration.

3. Economy and Property

Agriculture in Bruson has changed surprisingly little since the beginning of this century with respect to overall land use, extent and diversity of a household's farming enterprise, and even the kind of crops grown. The major changes have been rather in a declining emphasis on agriculture within the total economic picture. Today, for example, only about half of all men over twenty depend to any degree on agriculture for income. Of these, about sixty percent give *agriculteur* as either their sole or their principal occupation, and almost all these men are over fifty. For the rest, agriculture is a secondary occupation—with respect both to time and to income.

Of those men who do not consider themselves agriculteurs occupationally—deriving their incomes from a variety of *métiers* (trades—that is, occupations based on a standardized program of training and apprenticeship) or working as *ouvriers*, or laborers—most still engage in the minimal agricultural activity required to provide food staples for the household. Of the seventy-five households in Bruson, fifty are members of the *laiterie*. This means that they keep at least one or two milking cows, and harvest enough hay and forage crops (potatoes, beets, and rutabagas) to maintain the cows without the additional expense of buying commercial feed products.

The cows are of Hérens variety (named for the Valaisan

valley in which it originated)—reddish- to dark-brown, horned, short, muscular, heavy, and sure-footed. Well-adapted physically to the mountain environment, they are inferior in milk yield to other Swiss varieties. The variety is considered *bélliqueux* (war-like) in temperament, and a number of Bagnards breed one or two *reines à cornes* (queens with horns) for the *matches des reines*—contests between reines—which take place traditionally on the first days in the *alpages* and evoke great interest.

The cows are kept in village stables all winter, from November to early May. Husband and wife normally divide the labor of twice-daily milking, preparation and distribution of fodder, and cleaning of the stable. Keeping a pig or two does not appreciably increase the amount of labor or expense required and offers certain dividends to the household: the pigs consume the *petit lait* (whey) which has no commercial or human-nutritional value; they also provide the family with meat, since they are butchered at the end of the season and the meat stored in a community freezer. Because a good milker may cost as much as 2,000 francs if bought in the market, households do their own cattle breeding, keeping one or two heifers or yearlings in addition to their milkers, and even engage in a limited marketing of calves—selling the males which the household does not require for its own consumption.

In early May, the cattle are allowed to graze in pastures near the village, returning to the village stables every evening. Later in the month they are taken to the *mayens* for a period of two weeks (mayen actually means "May pasture"), and one or two members of the household—often a mother and child— remain there with the cows. In the early part of June, all the village cattle ascend from the mayens to the alpages, where they remain—in the care of the cooperative *consortage*—until late September. During that period, the household is deprived of the fresh milk to which it is accustomed, and many households keep a goat to fill this gap and provide *le lait d'été* (summer milk). At the end of September, the cattle return to the mayens for a two-week period, in the charge of the individual households. In mid-October they are once again in the village stables, grazing daily in nearby pastures.

Clearly, then, keeping even a single cow to supply household needs engages the household in a rather extensive agricultural cycle, depending on familistic and cooperative labor to avoid monetary expense. The alpage period, far from being a vacation period, liberates members of the household to harvest hay for winter fodder. Since most of the men work at jobs outside the village—and the summer season is the busiest for most occupations—haying becomes the work of women and children, although men take some time off from their jobs to assist in the heavier work of bringing in the hay. The forage crops must also be tended to—preparing the fields in early spring, planting, weeding, spraying insecticide, and harvesting.

In sum, while most Bruson men are ouvriers or practice métiers, most Bruson women are agriculteurs. Of seventeen women who have an occupation other than *ménagère* (housewife), twelve are young and unmarried. The five married women include the village mail carrier, the two shopkeepers, and the two café owners—the last four being engaged in family enterprises. Of these five households, only one is not also engaged in agriculture.

This picture of agricultural activity today is essentially the same as that of thirty years ago and earlier. At both times, the typical household kept two or three milking cows, a few additional heifers, yearlings, and calves, one or two pigs, and a goat. The traditional pack-animals (horses and mules) have been replaced by two-wheeled motorized farm machines, which somewhat alleviate the arduous labor of the traditional "third pack-animal"—as popular saying has it—the woman. The pattern of land use is also substantially the same: of the average land-holding of about 2.5 hectares (about six acres), a little over 80 percent is devoted to pasture and hayfield, and about 7 percent is planted to forage crops, small kitchen gardens, and just enough grapes to yield the approximately 300 liters of wine required annually for household consumption. It is in the remaining 10 percent of the land that one observes major differences. In the traditional economy of the nineteenth and early twentieth centuries, most of this land was planted to cereals—especially rye and wheat—to an altitude of 1,600 meters. About 1930, strawberries were introduced as a cash crop. By 1939 they accounted for about 6 percent of cultivable land. During the Second World War, most of this land returned to cereals, but today strawberries and the recently-introduced raspberries occupy 10 percent of all arable land (Andan 1965:54, Suter 1944:80).

The period around 1930 may be taken as a base-line for the modern Brusonin economy: subsistence-level grain cultivation began to give way to cash-cropping of strawberries; the cooperative Syndicate of Fruits and Vegetables was organized for spraying and marketing; in 1929, the present laiterie was founded, consolidating several smaller ones and putting the operation on a sounder financial basis. While the cash crops today account for 30 percent of the agricultural income of the village—a very productive industry considering that only 10 percent of the land is used—a modernized version of the traditional industry of dairying, especially the production of the famous Bagnes cheese, provides the remaining 70 percent. From the point of view of a household, however, all this agricultural income is merely supplementary to income earned in non-agricultural pursuits. The economy has shifted from self-sustaining agriculture to a rather high degree of dependence on the outside world.

The agricultural enterprise in Bruson is labor- and land-intensive. It is founded on private ownership of property and a familistic work-force. The Brusonin is subsistence- rather than profit-oriented, desiring only to provide well for his family, but modern standards of subsistence are high. The Swiss policy of political neutrality, by striving to maintain the peasant population, has actually resulted in raising farm prices above the Common Market level. In spite of protective tariffs, therefore, the Swiss consumer prefers to buy non-Swiss produce. At the same time, the heavily-subsidized Swiss peasant overproduces certain foods, further devaluing his labor. For him, the net result is that the proceeds of his labor have not kept up with the increasing cost of living.

Responsible for a large part of this cost of living is the modern ideal of *promotion scolaire* (educational advancement). Parents today encourage their children to take up métiers—not only because of a general respect for education but also as an avenue for improvement of living conditions, through higher and more regular incomes without the hazards and uncertainties of mountain agriculture. Once working at a métier, however, a man is no longer *"indépendent."* In order to find work, he may be forced to move out of the village—renting housing and buying nourishment. If it is possible to remain in the village and commute to his job, his time is not his own, and he depends heavily on his wife and children to maintain a minimal supplementary agriculture—which is financially essential for supporting and educating these children.

This complex situation which engenders heavy dependence on the larger society is also highly threatening to the peasant identity of the Brusonin. The word *paysan* invokes a constellation of meanings and implications, chief among which are these two: that a paysan is someone who works the land (implying an emotional attachment to it), and that the land is *his* land.

Discussions, in Bruson, about occupations and career possibilities are structured in terms of three general categories: *paysan, paysan-ouvrier,* and *ouvrier-paysan.* The first of these belongs to the past but remains an ideal for the present and future. Few men today, as I have shown, are paysans by occupation—but all believe in the essential goodness and rightness of the paysan mentality—*la sagesse paysanne* (peasant wisdom), as one informant expressed it, pointing out that Pope John XXIII had this quality and was not even a Brusonin. The distinction between paysan-ouvrier and ouvrier-paysan is made on the basis of relative freedom—to be called an ouvrier-paysan is mildly demeaning and patronizing—and freedom depends essentially on property ownership.

This distinction is clarified and dramatized in the history of the present alpage organization. During my first few months of fieldwork, I tried to discover the difference between mayen and alpage, seeking it in such physical features as relative altitude, quality of the grass, and location of the timber-line. The response to my questioning, in these terms, was confusing and inconclusive. Finally I learned what differentiates these two kinds of land to a Brusonin: the mayen is privately owned, and the alpage belongs to the *bourgeoisie.* Further distinguishing features are based on these two. For example, mayen land is fertilized chemically as well as through grazing, yielding more hay. This higher productivity of mayen land over the alpage is explained as being the result of private ownership: one takes better care of one's own property than of community property, since one has a direct interest in it. This widespread belief—together with the reluctance to make capital investments in the traditionally labor-intensive agriculture—explains the violent opposition of almost all Brusonins to any suggestions for increasing agricultural proceeds through the use of communal facilities and labor. Economic cooperation is acceptable only on a very limited scale.

The two consortages of Bruson are the oldest of the economic cooperatives. Each one uses its own alpage—named for the mountains rising above Bruson, Mille and Six-Blanc. Before the 1930s, the consortages were loosely organized cooperatives with the primary function of holding usufructory rights to the bourgeois-owned lands. The members—*consorts*—shared the major work responsibilities but looked after their own cattle and made their own cheeses. Most of the shared work consisted of repairing the damages—sometimes very severe—caused by natural forces: the pastures and streams had to be cleared annually of rocks and debris, the grass weeded, and the roads repaired.

By the 1930s, however, a major problem developed: the milk yield was being reduced because of over-grazing and a too-short grazing season. The consortages were forced to make the drastic decision of enlarging the alpages by buying up parcels of contiguous mayen land. This step provided more pasture for the herds and also a longer alpage season, since the newly-acquired land was at a lower altitude. In addition, other improvements were made resulting in a more highly organized and cooperative system: community stables and other necessary structures were built in the alpages; maintenance of the land and buildings and care of the cows devolved upon a small group of alpage personnel, headed by a *maître-berger* (chief cowherd); and cheese was now made communally by a specialized *fromager*.

Two major benefits resulted from this drastic action of converting private property into community property: first, the alpage became a more profitable venture—increasing the milk yield of the herd with a decrease in human labor, and improving the reliability of the cheeses through the employment of a specialist; secondly, the large majority of Brusonins who were not employed in the alpage were free to cultivate their lands,

especially those planted to the newly-introduced and highly
profitable strawberries.

There were also problems associated with the enlargement
of the alpages. The loss of mayen land meant the loss of a
certain amount of the hay crop. After much resistance, the
consorts finally decided to reduce the herd by about 30 percent
—solving this problem as well as the one of over-grazing.
Another difficulty, more subtle and insidious than these, had
to do with staffing the alpages. As Brusonins were freed to
work in their fields during this busy period, and as this work
became more profitable through the cultivation of strawberries,
it became more difficult to find alpage personnel. The jobs of
maître-berger and fromager are peasant vocations. In this
period, however, the peasants were either turning to more
intensive cultivation of market crops or becoming paysan-
ouvriers and accepting outside wage-labor. Those who could
be found to work in the alpages had to be paid higher salaries,
and the cost of keeping cows in the alpages began to rise.

The alpages today are no longer profit-producing and barely
manage to equalize cost and yield. They are, however, considered a "necessary evil," because they remove the cattle from
the village at a season when villagers are heavily charged with
profit-producing labor, both agricultural and otherwise. The
revolutionary step taken in the 1930s of enlarging the alpages
by converting private property into community property was
an attempt to optimize the major subsistence base of the time,
dairying—that is, to maintain the traditional economy by carefully manipulating the traditional social structure. The ultimate effect, however, contributed to the creation of
market-dependent paysans and of paysan-ouvriers—a transformation of the entire socio-economic structure as traditionally
constituted.

What has not been altered by this history of irreversible
adaptations is the ideological system expressed in the phrase
"la sagesse paysanne." In keeping with this ideology of freedom
based on private ownership of property, Brusonins today are
extremely suspicious and wary of all cooperative enterprises.
When they speak of *communauté* (community), they have in
mind a voluntary society composed of free agents—in other
words, a Confederation. It is in this sense that they use the

word communauté in nostalgic descriptions of the early days
of the alpages, before the inevitable effects became visible:
"L'alpage—c'était la plus belle communauté que nous avions."
(The alpage—that was the most beautiful community we had.)

Part II

The Ménage

4. The Meaning of Ménage

Two hundred and fifty people live in Bruson, approximately half of them in the adult productive years of their lives—that is, between twenty and fifty years. A little over one-quarter of the total are under twenty, and a little under a quarter are over sixty. (See Figure 1.) This is the age distribution of a fairly stable population. The distribution of people by sex, however, presents an interestingly skewed picture. While there is a slight preponderance of men over women on the whole—55 percent to 45 percent—in the age group twenty-sixty there are about three men for every two women. Even more striking is the fact that, in this age group, there are about three unmarried men for every unmarried woman. Thus, within the space of a single paragraph, we have already stumbled upon one major irregularity in the demography of Bruson.

Although drawing broad demographic outlines provides a useful starting point, greater analytic interest lies in studying exceptional cases. By taking a more distant view, generalizations specific to Bruson—dependent on the cultural context —emerge. Close examination then reveals each family, each household, as an exceptional case.

The word *famille*, for example, is seldom heard in Bruson. The concept of nuclear family exists, but the actual group is

31

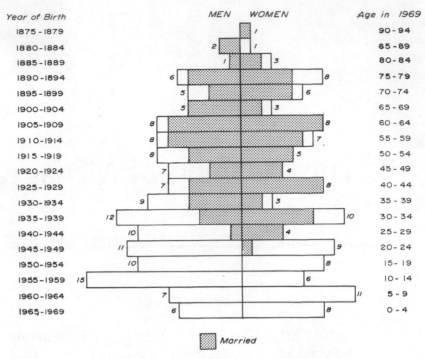

Year of Birth	MEN	WOMEN	Age in 1969
1875-1879		1	90-94
1880-1884	2	1	85-89
1885-1889	1	3	80-84
1890-1894	6	8	75-79
1895-1899	5	6	70-74
1900-1904	5	3	65-69
1905-1909	8	8	60-64
1910-1914	8	7	55-59
1915-1919	8	5	50-54
1920-1924	7	4	45-49
1925-1929	7	8	40-44
1930-1934	9	3	35-39
1935-1939	12	10	30-34
1940-1944	10	4	25-29
1945-1949	11	9	20-24
1950-1954	10	8	15-19
1955-1959	15	6	10-14
1960-1964	7	11	5-9
1965-1969	6	8	0-4

▨ Married

Figure 1. Age-Sex-Marital Status Distribution.

most often found in a *ménage*, or household. A ménage is defined by Brusonins as a group of people who regularly produce, prepare, and consume food together—*faire le ménage ensemble*. It is conceived as an economic, not a kinship, unit. The definition never makes any reference to kinship relations within this group, but, in most cases, the group is some form of what we call the nuclear family or the extended family—that is, parents and their unmarried children, with the possible addition of another lineal relative such as a grandparent in the extended family case. Of the 250 Brusonins, three-quarters live in this kind of unit—that is, one that includes lineally related members of at least two generations. There are 75 ménages in all, of which two-thirds are of this type.

The concept ménage, then, is a narrowing of the concept "family," since it normally excludes all siblings except those of the youngest generation present. The ménage is seen from within, from the viewpoint of members of that youngest generation—the children. The siblings of the parents become "Aunt" and "Uncle" to the children and live in ménages of their own, as parents to the "cousins" of the children. There are, in fact, only two ménages of the extended family type in which the additional relative is a parent's sibling. One of these consists of a childless couple and the husband's unmarried brother. The brother had been living alone until 1968 when the couple returned to Bruson from another canton in order to join forces with him in establishing a new café. The other family consists of a widowed mother, her children, and her unmarried brother. This brother and sister had previously lived in separate apartments in their father's house and joined to form a single ménage only after the death of the sister's husband.

These two exceptional ménages illustrate a refinement of the definition of the term: members of a ménage *usually* live under the same roof but *always* share a single kitchen. The strength of this rule is demonstrated by some extreme cases encompassed by it. In one case, a nuclear family shares a house with the mother's mother, but they function as separate ménages—that is, there are two kitchens. In another case, a nuclear family consisting of parents and their eight children is housed in three separate apartments located in two separate houses which are in different *quartiers*. Two of the apartments are "where the children sleep"—that is, all but the two youngest who are housed with the parents. The family comes together to eat in the third apartment where the parents sleep. The existence of three separate dwellings for this ménage is considered a necessity because of its size. The essential feature of ménage is also well demonstrated by a temporary expulsion from the eating table of two of the sons whose public antisocial behavior had become insupportable to the mother. Short of disinheriting them—and this is a poor family with no property—she could only "throw them out." In Bruson, to be "thrown out" is to be denied the family table. "They sleep in the apartment, and I wash their laundry, but I won't have them at the table," was the mother's explanation.

The ménage is defined economically by its use of a common kitchen where food is prepared and consumed in common. The production of this food, however, presents an ambiguity which is often exploited by husband and wife. Swiss law requires the joining of properties upon marriage and regards this common property base as unitary for all purposes including taxation, sale, and inheritance.

In Bruson, the husband is informally acknowledged as manager of all the ménage property—in his role as *chef de l'exploitation*. Brusonins, however, continue to identify a particular field or vineyard as "coming from" either husband or wife. Further, the transfer of ménage property to the heirs sometimes takes place on two separate occasions—one *partage* for property which "comes from" the husband and another for the wife's contribution. This treatment of ménage property as if it were separately owned is legally invisible since only the results of the partage are recorded.

The legal and the cognitive systems coexist without friction. In addition, the contrast between them is used to clarify certain unusual ménage situations, especially those which seem to violate the legal requirement of commonality of property. In one case, the legal-cognitive ambiguity was used to explain a wife's apparent lack of grief upon her husband's death: immediately after the funeral, she returned to her work in the fields, chatting and joking as usual with neighbors and passersby. No one seemed surprised at her behavior. This conjugal relationship had always been a strange one, was the explanation: in fact, there were years when she didn't even work her husband's land but only that which he had transferred to her children. This woman married into Bruson from a nearby valley, thus bringing no real property into the marriage. Perhaps, for this reason, she never felt properly married since the ménage was a one-sided creation economically, lacking that essential feature of joining properties and considering them as one.

In another case, both the legal and the cognitive understandings of the concept of ménage property are used to clarify a particular situation. The situation involves a family consisting of six children—three daughters, all married and living in Bruson or Le Sappey, and three unmarried sons, all living with the parents. The mother has already apportioned her property and signed it over to the children. The father, however, has not done so. If he fails to "make the partage" before his death, the property automatically goes into *hoirie*—that is, it is owned jointly by all the children and inalienable by any one of them without the consent of all the others. As delicate as is a partage made before a parent's death—almost invariably leading to quarrels among the heirs—the hoirie situation is even more troublesome since all heirs are bound to act only in unanimity. This father is now "too old to work the land." By refusing to apportion it among his children, he maintains the original economic ménage and retains his position as chef de l'exploitation, with his sons—all over forty—working for him and completely dependent on him.

This family fulfills to the letter every condition of ménage, but it is regarded as something less than an ideal ménage. It is not considered normal for a father to remain chef de l'exploitation beyond his productive years, for grown sons to continue to behave as economically dependent children, for married daughters to have nothing to do with their family of orientation. What is lacking is a certain spirit of continuity: the ménage, like everything else in life, must evolve, is the general opinion.

Ideally, ménage continuity leads to the creation of a new social unit which I will call the converging family. The converging family is composed of two ménages, related lineally as parent and child, which act as a single ménage with respect to food production. This unit comes into being upon the marriage of a child. At this point, the parents are still productive and have probably not yet decided how the ménage property will be divided among the children. Thus, the father remains chef de l'exploitation of the parent ménage. The newly married son (or son-in-law) becomes *chef de famille* of the new ménage —a rather vague term which may be translated as "the man of the house." Authority is vested in him, but it is an incomplete authority since he does not yet control his own property. This fledgling ménage does not have a property base of its own, but it does function as a common and exclusive unit with respect to food preparation and consumption. The son (or daughter) continues to work the parental lands and to participate in the food production of the parents' ménage. The spouse does the same, to the extent that this is possible. Thus, a daughter-in-law will spend most of her time working at agriculture with her husband's parents, while a son-in-law, who may have a job outside the village, will help when he has or can take free time from his job—particularly at times of exceptionally heavy agricultural work such as the harvest. If both

young people are from Bruson, then the young ménage will
be involved in two converging family units, working equally
with the ménages of both sets of parents.

Although there may be occasional housekeeping and dining
in common between the older and younger ménages—invitations
to dinner, gift-giving of homemade food products, assistance
with housecleaning—it is noteworthy that these occasions are
completely reciprocal and that there is in them no violation
of either ménage as a discrete gastronomic unit.

Whatever its size or composition, and regardless of its current
degree of economic independence, the ménage is always treated
as a discrete gastronomic unit in the social structure. The
never-married and widowed people living alone prepare and
eat their food alone. In those few ménages consisting of two
individuals—two unmarried adults or a married couple—the two
prepare and eat their food together. The nuclear and extended
families—whether young and still participating in food production with the parent ménages, or established with their own
property base—prepare and eat their food as a single unit.

While there is considerable variation in post-marital residence patterns, depending largely on the special circumstances
in the particular case, there is strict adherence to a rule of
neogastrolocality: a new ménage must have its own kitchen.
The young couple may move into an apartment that is the
property of one set of parents or the other. Couples with growing
children try to provide for this by improving or enlarging their
houses, building separate apartments within. Lacking this possibility, the young couple may rent an apartment in the
village—although there are few such apartments available—
while saving money to build their own house or renovate an
existing one on family property. Or they will move out of the
village and rent an apartment in Le Châble, in Martigny, or
wherever is most convenient. Being a tenant is considered one
of the most fundamental threats to a man's freedom, but it
is preferable in the long run to "living with" his or his wife's
parents—that is, in a common ménage with them. One young
couple tried this, living with the husband's parents until they
had three children. Then suddenly, but not surprisingly to a
Brusonin, they moved out and now live in another canton,
never communicating with the parents. "They were always

quarreling with the parents," says a young woman who knew them well.

In this study, I shall use the native term "ménage" for the most part, rather than glossing it as "household" or "domestic group." Neither of these standard terms adequately describes the Brusonin unit. The first, "household," suggests co-residence which, as I have shown, is not a necessary feature of the ménage. The second, "domestic group," seems closer in implication to what I am calling the "converging family." The ménage, a unit created by marriage and based on a residence rule of neogastro-locality, is defined by common and exclusive commensality and by its relations with the two families of orientation of its founders in the converging family.

5. Economic Gastronomy

Under normal circumstances, a *ménage* eats together and excludes non-members from its table. But eating and drinking also serve important functions in the larger society of the village and beyond. They are binding events in an economic and social network. As such, they mimic the gastronomic unity of the *ménage* since they constitute prescribed trespasses on its gastronomic inviolability.

The particular form taken by such events depends on two factors: the sex of the participants, and the content of the event, which I will classify broadly as economic, social, or ritual. Men and women generally participate in quite different and separate spheres of activity; even when both participate in the same kind of activity, they rarely do so at the same time. Generally speaking, women confine themselves to the private arenas of behavior—especially the home—while men participate in the public arena—the café, for instance; with respect to content, women are generally more active in the religious sphere and men in the secular. In considering events which are extensions of the ménage principle, one can combine these three classification systems—content, site, and sex. Thus, economic events are secular, typically occur in the public arena, and involve male participation. Certain social events, although secular, take place in the woman's arena of the home. Ritual

events, all are fundamentally dependent on the ménage principle—the solidarity and exclusivity of a group as revealed in
they are restricted to men.

Whatever the content, site, or sexual restrictions of these
events, all are fundamentally dependent on the ménage principle—the solidarity and exclusivity of a group as revealed in
eating and drinking behavior. Such an event is, first of all,
gastronomic—involving eating and/or drinking; secondly, the
group participating in the event is not an actual ménage
group—that is, it does not regularly and jointly participate in
food production, preparation, and consumption. These events,
which are gastronomic but take place outside the limits of a
ménage, utilize the gastronomic ménage principle in order to
simulate ménage solidarity.

Economic gastronomy depends upon the fact that the Brusonin does not like to be indebted to anyone. He sees himself
as free and without obligations—owner of his home and lands;
manager, foreman, and laborer in his agricultural enterprise.
If he accepts wages for his labor, it is always from an outsider,
for work done outside his own village, usually seasonal work
paid on an hourly basis. If he has a *métier* he is proud because
this skill becomes part of his personal capital. If he works as
an unskilled laborer to supplement his agricultural earnings,
he calls himself a *paysanouvrier*—carefully explaining that the
emphasis is on *paysan* and thus retaining his self-image as a
free man.

The desire for freedom from obligation tends to sensitize him
to any situation which might involve an imbalance and thus
create an inequality in his relations with a member of his own
community. Within the community, there are two governing
principles: "*nous sommes tous égaux*" ("we are all equal"), and
"we are like one family." Here is an interesting and rare usage
of the word *famille* as an amorphous but stable group of
individuals who are related but for whom the precise lines
and degrees of kinship need not be known or specified. The
group is not an economic unit like the ménage. It is based
on kinship, both in the specific and in the general sense: the
belief that "relatedness" exists leads to the expectation of a
certain kind of behavior, whereby each individual is a separate
entity standing on an equal footing with all other individuals.

No one is better—though some are more religious (*plus prati-quant*); no one is richer—though some are "more comfortable" (*plus aisé*); no one is smarter—though some are more educated (*plus instruit*). There are no creditors or debtors, since every situation that threatens to create them is dissolved by almost immediate reciprocity.

At this point, the concept of equality diverges sharply from the concept of "one family." Or perhaps it would be better to say that the meaning of "family" as distinct from "ménage" becomes suddenly clear. Within a ménage, it is impossible to incur debts, because each member has clearly stated duties to fulfill as his contribution to the ménage. He is, in the last analysis, acting for himself, for his own advantage. But, at the level of the village community, an individual is free and may continue to act always only in his own direct interest. If he goes one step out of his way to be of service to someone else, he is behaving in the spirit of "one family," but his action must be reciprocated or else the recipient's freedom is threatened, his equality within the "family" is undermined.

Since this is an event in the context of "family," the reciprocity must take the form of a currency acceptable in a family. Money is a commercial currency used in impersonal transactions with strangers. Food and drink, however, are not normally negotiable items in the larger world. In a farming and wine-growing village, they are not even particularly valuable items, since each man potentially produces his own. For these reasons, food and drink are the ideal currency within the familistic village community. Payment for a service is uncalculated; it is, indeed, only a token payment symbolizing the annulment of the debt. *Je te paye un verre*—I'll buy you a drink—is one of the most frequently heard phrases in Bruson.

This form of reciprocity accomplishes more than just canceling the debt. As the idiom of food and drink is directly tied to the concept of ménage, the debtor is symbolically opening his ménage to the creditor, allowing him momentarily to enter that closed domain where he, the debtor, is master. Thus, he not only obliterates his previously subordinate position as a man in debt, but he adopts the superordinate position of host.

Payer un verre is the appropriate gesture of reciprocity for small services rendered by fellow villagers, whether these services have been requested or are offered spontaneously. In either case, they are non-professional and extraordinary services, and the service-payment incident is limited to two or perhaps three persons. The service is rendered in the spirit of "one family" and is reciprocated in the gastronomic currency of the ménage. A passerby stops on his way home to help a man unload his winter's wood supply. A neighbor with a car, going to Martigny, is asked to pick up a package there. These services are non-professional in that they depend on no special skill, only on circumstances; they are extraordinary in that they do not occur regularly—at least not between the same two persons.

If a professional service is requested, payment is usually made in the commercial currency of money, and the donor gives his service in his capacity as employee in an extra-village enterprise. Thus, one's neighbor the carpenter is asked to repair a loose molding. He does so as an employee of the carpentry firm in Le Châble and charges a standard fee. When the job is done, however, he is invited to have a drink—*allons boire un verre*. This is not payment—payer un verre—since the service will be paid for in the professional, commercial, extra-village sphere. It is, in fact, a gesture intended to negate the payment, to remove the service from that sphere and place it in the "one family" sphere. The participants are reminding each other that they are kinsmen, and not tradesman and client. If, on the other hand, one's neighbor the carpenter is visiting, on his way home from work, and offers to repair the molding, does so immediately, quickly, and perhaps with help from his host—this service is in the "one family" spirit and must be reciprocated, either in the form payer un verre or allons boire un verre.

A service requiring more time or inconvenience on the part of the donor has exceeded the range of small service, and payment in the form of a drink is no longer adequate. Payment then is made in kind—in labor. A villager helps another bring in his hay harvest; the latter reciprocates by milking his cows a few evenings when he must work late. Agricultural work, however, approaches the professional sphere since it is income-producing. Thus, certain agriculturally-related services are paid for in commercial currency, money—always softened by "having

a drink" (allons boire un verre). One villager, for example, owns
a jeep which he operates as a taxi service. For a standard fee,
he helps someone transport manure to his fields.

Whatever form the payment may take—money, a drink,
labor—a service-payment relationship in the agricultural area
tends to become regularized between a particular pair of individuals or ménages, and, in so doing, it becomes less a commercial relationship than a "one family" mutual-aid relationship.
Since everyday agricultural activity is largely in the hands of
women, and since women do not normally operate either in
the commercial or in the public sphere, it is natural that such
exchanges of services are paid for in kind—either in the home
itself or in the fields as extensions of the home. A woman helps
another in haying and expects, in return, help with her strawberry harvest. Payment, here, is calculated on the basis of need
rather than in the neutral currency of money. A certain
bachelor often helps his neighbor at heavy agricultural tasks;
in return—on each specific occasion—the neighbor's wife invites
him to a meal.

These are all forms of more or less overt payment, using
the currency of the ménage, for services rendered in the idiom
of "one family." Food and drink also occur as "gifts"—forms
of covert payment. In these situations, too, the ménage is
symbolically opened to admit an outsider, the result being a
return to equality after a moment of imbalance. As in cases
of overt payment, here too the "'gift" is to some extent person-
alized to the wants or needs of the recipient; in general, it
takes the form of drink among men, food among women.

An example of this form of covert payment concerns the
village *fromager*. He is a paid employee of the cooperative
laiterie. His normal duties include the processing of milk to
manufacture cheese and the preparation of cream to be sold
to the central laiterie in Sion. When a special service is requested of him by one of the members of the cooperative—a liter
of cream for home use, for example—it is customary to bring
him a "gift" of a bottle of wine when the service is performed—
when the cream is picked up. Of course, the cream is paid for,
its monetary value deducted from the member's account, but
the "gift" of wine is more important. Setting aside the cream
for this member is a special service which goes beyond the

requirements of the fromager's professional duties. The member is, thus, specially indebted to the fromager and erases the debt in the usual manner, in the ménage idiom. This being a relationship between men, the proper payment is wine. The fromager immediately opens the bottle and shares it with the member and any other men present. This action further removes the event from any possible commercial interpretation. The fromager reassures the member that his "gift" has been accepted in the desired spirit. At the same time, he also turns the table on the member and puts himself, the fromager, in the position of host. The entire transaction has occurred in open violation of Rule Number 24 of the Statutes of the Laiterie: "there shall be no alcoholic beverages in the laiterie."

Women, too, are involved in economic events which draw on the ménage principle of gastronomic exclusivity, though to a lesser extent than are men. These involvements differ not only in degree but in kind. Women, being more limited than men in their spheres of activity, tend to form regular service-payment relationships with each other, usually within the circle of relatives or within the *quartier*. These standing relationships of mutual aid are not quite the same as the casual, spontaneous service-payment incidents in which men find themselves. As among men, the service is non-professional and causes minimal inconvenience or effort to the donor. The payment, as among men, is usually based on one's own resources and on the special needs of the other. In these standing relationships, however, women do not think in terms of "payment" but in terms of "replacement" for a service rendered. The concept of compensation is present but couched in covert terms of gift-giving. The payment concept may be expressed more overtly when the event is outside the scope of a standing mutual-aid relationship —that is, when it occurs only once or rarely, and between women who are not regularly in such a relationship.

To illustrate this difference between overt "payment" and covert "gift-giving" or "replacement," I shall consider one village woman, Rosy, in several relationships, all of them rather typical. Rosy and Marcelle, both in their early thirties, are quartier neighbors. They are distant cousins but do not think of each other as kin; they often play cards together, in a café group, but do not regard each other as particular friends. Rosy

regularly sets Marcelle's hair. Marcelle invites Rosy to "help
yourself to my garden." When one woman has finished her
day's haying, she may give the other a hand. There is this
kind of continuous interaction between them. Their relationship is not a friendship, nor is it based on imagined kinship
obligations. It is purely and simply a standing relationship of
mutual aid. The men of the two ménages also become involved
in the relationship: Rosy's father helps Marcelle with milking
when her husband must work late at his job; Marcelle's husband helps unload the barrels of new wine that Rosy's husband
has brought up from the vineyards in Fully.

Rosy and Suzanne have more in common personally—they
are about the same age, childless, and operate cafés. They are
not related, Suzanne having come to Bruson only after her
marriage, and they live far apart—Rosy in the village, and
Suzanne in her café on the ski slopes above the village. All
these factors of similarity and difference make the two women
useful to each other. Suzanne, coming from a big city, drives
a car and regularly takes Rosy with her to Martigny, where
they shop and go to the hairdresser's. Rosy, being in the village,
receives Suzanne's mail and holds it for her. Suzanne and her
husband often have supper in Rosy's café and are occasionally
invited to a meal or snack in her own kitchen. The two husbands
work together on the ski slopes.

Although the content of the two relationships is quite different—the first being oriented to the agricultural and neighborly sphere and the second to the modern commercial life—
they are both essentially standing relationships of mutual aid,
initiated and maintained by the women but allowing the
possibility of male inclusion.

Rosy also participates in extraordinary events of service and
payment in which the payment aspect is overt and explicit.
She spends a morning harvesting strawberries with a woman
neighbor who has given her an afternoon's help in haying. When
I gave her a ride to Martigny one day, she insisted on paying
for our coffee and snack there—"because you drove me down."
When she sends a neighborhood child to the store for groceries,
she always tells him to buy himself some candy at the store,
or gives him some of the small change when he returns.

Both the standing relationships and these extraordinary

events illustrate the avoidance of debt and the use of food and drink to restore the balance. Women, like men, are members of discrete ménages, defined by gastronomic exclusivity, and also participate in the "one family" that is the village. There are important differences, however, between men and women with respect to the ménage and the village "family." Women are much more strongly identified with the ménage than are men; they are much more confined in their daily activities and interpersonal contacts to the private arena of house and fields. Their freedom of movement within the larger social structure of village and beyond is severely restricted. Their time is spent at housework, child-care, agricultural work in season, and kitchen visiting within a small regular circle during the "dead season" of winter. They are, in effect, living the traditional village life of a hundred years ago, while their husbands and sons have become articulated with the modern world.

This subculture of women is based on a subsistence economy, in which money is a rare and unusual medium of payment. The ménage, from this point of view, is ideally a self-sufficient socio-economic unit; through its participation in standing mutual-aid relationships with other like units, it is part of a larger self-sufficient unit, the quartier; the ménage also participates in the still larger unit of the village. Today, there is only a vague remembrance of the quartier as a socio-economic unit; for most purposes, it is bypassed in favor of the village, which is "one family." Since the village is no longer isolated from other villages in the valley, it is now less a working active unit and more a symbol to which loyalty is attached. The ménage, of course, continues to demand one's loyalty, and thus arises a certain conflict between ménage and village. But the ménage also continues to be a functioning unit, not essentially different from what it was a hundred years ago. Thus, the woman, whose daily activity is centered upon and confined to the ménage, has largely retained her traditional and clearly defined role: she functions comfortably within the traditional sphere of ménage-quartier-village and has a minimum of loyalty conflict problems. She forms standing relationships of mutual-aid; she pays her debts, as they are incurred, through "replacement" of services or "gift-giving" of goods. When she uses money as a medium of payment, she does so with some discomfort and self-consciousness—as if she is imitating men and momentarily stepping into their world. For her, the ménage is everyday life, and not a symbolic transformation of some fading reality.

6. Women in Commerce

Modern life has made more of a direct incursion on some *ménages* than on others. In those ménages, the woman's daily economic behavior has been modified. Here is a hybrid form of the traditional and the modern. Women behave like men, and the use of the ménage principle as a social stabilizer is in force again. It is significant that the four independent business enterprises located in the village, though in some cases technically owned or managed by men, are actually operated by women. These women are not violating any cultural rules for their sex; on the contrary, they are fulfilling their duties to husband and ménage. In these cases, however, their traditional agricultural duties have been more or less supplanted by modern commercial tasks.

The enterprises in question are the two village cafés and the two *épiceries*. The women have occupations other than *ménagère*: two are *cafetiers* and two are *commerçantes*. Since these are family enterprises, actually located in the house, these women combine their household and commercial duties with ease. They are permitted to enter the male worlds of café or business, but their participation is defined in terms of their duties as women to contribute to the common economic enterprise of the ménage. It is, in fact, duty and not choice that puts them in this non-traditional setting. Once there, however, they must abide by its principles and rules. These women must deal with the delicate balance between individualism and community, and they do so in the same way as men. In the intra-village commercial relationship, the entrepreneur and the customer (or the employer and employee) have a common goal: to preserve their independence within the framework of "one family." Both make strong efforts to minimize the commercial aspect of the relationship—the customer by paying his debts as quickly and flamboyantly as possible, the entrepreneur by denying the existence of debt. They achieve these ends by using the idiom and currency of the ménage.

I was a regular customer at one of the cafés, taking most of my meals there during the nineteen-month period of field-work. At the same time, the proprietress, Rosy, and I became good friends. The history of this dual relationship will reveal some important aspects of the quality of village enterprises. My position was, of course, unusual from the villagers' point of view, but only in degree: although an outsider who would one day leave the village, I was considered and treated, during my residence, as "one of us."

I was the only customer of such regularity and long-standing to eat at the café—which was equipped only to serve beverages, simple meals of fondue or sandwiches, and occasional group dinners. To take lunch and supper at the café every day was, in a sense, equivalent to being a member of Rosy's ménage, since I belonged to no ménage of my own. But I was obviously not a member of that ménage: I did not eat at their table but in the café; I was not a relative; I was not even Swiss. In the eyes of the village at large, I was simply a paying customer who happened to be friendly with the proprietor—in other words, I was like any other Brusonin who frequented the café.

But Rosy and I knew that our relationship was much more intense than the typical business relationship she had with a fellow Brusonin. She cooked for me every day, even on Tuesdays, when the café was closed. On those evenings, she served my meal in the café, left me alone just long enough to eat it, and then—always awaiting my specific invitation—joined me for tea and extended conversation. With the exception of these Tuesday evenings, our business relationship and our friendship were quite separate. On many afternoons she worked with me as informant, within the friendship context. As the friendship developed and our relations became more comfortable, I would often visit her, in her kitchen, after having supper in the café. Starting in May, after five months in Bruson, I took only suppers at the café and ate more and more often at Rosy's family table in her kitchen. This became a regular practice except on weekends, when my husband arrived and we ate together in the café. I was still a paying customer, but now Rosy worried less about the variety or quality of meals she served me and showed disappointment when I had to miss a meal for some reason or had to leave immediately after eating. In July, Rosy and I began to use the familiar form of address, *tu*, with each other. Soon after, I was also on familiar terms with her husband Willy and her father, calling the latter "Papa," as did Rosy.

The distinction between "Madame" the customer and "Dany" the ménage member and friend had become blurred. Our business relationship remained businesslike but became more comfortable and, in fact, approximated more closely the comparable relationship Rosy had with her fellow villagers. We had established initially that I would pay for a month's meals at the end of the month, receiving a written bill. Although it was Rosy herself who kept the household accounts and calculated and wrote my bills, she always deferred in public to her husband Willy as the business manager. In the early months of my residence, it was he who presented the bill and whom I paid. On these occasions, he either apologized for the "large" amount of the bill or verbosely explained the justness of it by quoting current meat prices to me. It was he too, as *patron* of the café, who every week or two made the hospitality gesture of buying drinks for my husband and me—that is, denying the business relationship through the ménage idiom of drink.

The monthly bill also became an instrument for denial of our business relationship. It was always I who had to request the bill, and there was always a time lag of at least one week between the request and the presentation. Furthermore, Rosy and Willy both were upset if I tried to pay the bill upon receipt, insisting that "there is no hurry." This was the case even when

I was about to leave the village for a short period. In fact, on such occasions, it was almost impossible for me to pay before leaving. The bill was thus dismissed as something very minor and incidental in our relationship. Rosy and Willy would insist that I was, after all, coming back—something of which they could not be sure, given their very limited contact with and understanding of the larger world. It was clear, however, that they were imparting to me their own culture's values with regard to indebtedness and paying me a compliment—implying, in effect, that I, as a good person, would pay my bills. This became explicit on one particular occasion when I teased Rosy about leaving town with the unpaid bill and never returning. She responded, half-jokingly, that that was why she wouldn't let me pay before leaving—to insure my return.

When I went back to Geneva, it was often with commissions for Rosy. I would bring back the requested item, and she would pay me for it. Sometimes I brought back small gifts for her and the others in the household. These gifts—a small slide viewer, some fancy bottle corks—were accepted with pleasure but caused some puzzlement. This can be understood in the context of gift-giving as covert payment: I had already paid for services, so there was no need to make "gifts." When, however, the gift was a food item—a chocolate bar, for instance —no one was baffled, since food was part of the traditional currency, and the event was comparable to Rosy's standing invitation from her friend Marcelle to "help yourself to my garden." Photographs I gave were also accepted in this way, since they were direct products of my work.

Such a comfortable blend of business and friendship as this one is difficult to conceive of in our own urban culture where it is said explicitly that "business and friendship do not mix," that one will always tend to dominate and destroy the other. In a small community like Bruson, however, where people live at fairly close quarters and are, by their own admission, more or less distantly related to one another, such an overlap of spheres of interaction is highly desirable. Overlap is facilitated by the Brusonin's conceptual framework of the potential disharmony between his roles as ménage member and participant in the "one family" of the village: he is always striving to adjust imbalances by extending the ménage principle to intra-village commercial relationships. He uses the ménage idiom of food and drink to soften, if not to deny, a commercial relationship with his fellows.

The four women who operate commercial enterprises in the village are, at first glance, in a somewhat more difficult position than men, since they are required to enter the male arena of public economic behavior and to abide by its rules. In fact, however, they are the ideal entrepreneurs since they, as women, embody the ménage principle, and their extension of it to commercial situations seems completely natural. Ida, in her épicerie, happily extends credit to her customers, keeping a running record of purchases in a little notebook. As she does so, she momentarily steps out of her role as shopkeeper and becomes the customer's cousin or aunt, unquestioningly and trustingly making a small short-term loan for the customer's convenience rather than for his need. It is as if the customer had carelessly left his purse at home that day. The customer accepts the credit as he would accept a borrowed cup of sugar. On some future visit to the store, he will pay his accumulated bill without comment on either side. Ida also occasionally makes small gifts of chocolate to regular customers, ostensibly as a simple act of friendship. When business is slow, she may invite a customer to have coffee with her in the kitchen, at the rear of the store.

Both épiceries, at some time or another, require additional help—for instance, when there is a large group of skiers in the village, or when the commerçante is ill or has just had a baby. These occasions are of special interest because they are actually cases of standing mutual-aid relationships between women— that is, within the commercial sphere they duplicate women's traditional relationships. The helpers speak of "replacing" the shopkeepers—always on a temporary short-term basis—but the time and energy required remove this help from the domain of "small services" and require monetary payment. Each shop-keeper always enlists the help of the same individual, who, in turn, feels an obligation to do the service. The helper is not chosen on the basis of kinship or friendship, but is in both cases a woman of the same quartier who is relatively free to perform the service. One shopkeeper, a woman of forty, has a helper of twenty-two, a recently married girl who worked

in the store full-time before her marriage. The two are distantly
related, though neither can precisely describe the relationship.
In any case, they do not think of themselves as relatives or
as friends. They claim only close acquaintance, on the basis
of being neighbors and of working together. When the young
woman had her first baby, the shopkeeper was one of the group
of women who gave the baby a gift.

A similar situation obtains at the other épicerie, although,
in that case, the ages of the women are reversed: the shopkeeper
is a young married woman and her helper is a grandmother.
They live in the same quartier. They have the same family
name, and, upon questioning, concede that their husbands may
be distant cousins. Kinship, however, is not a factor in this
relationship, nor is friendship since they never interact in other
situations.

Rosy's café provides us with two additional employer-employee relationships that are of special interest. The first is
a regular and long-standing relationship between Rosy, as
proprietress, and Geneviève who works as *sommelière*, or bar-
maid, in the café. Geneviève is an unmarried girl of twenty-two
who lives with her parents, her sister, and two brothers in the
house across the street from the café. She has been Rosy's
sommelière since finishing *école ménagère* at the age of sixteen.
She works full time, six days a week, and receives a salary
in addition to customers' tips. On her working days, she eats
lunch and supper at Rosy's table. Her father and the older
of her two brothers are regular customers at the café, and both
parents come in about one evening a week to play cards with
others.

There is no known kinship tie between Rosy and Geneviève,
and, because of the difference in their age and marital status,
they do not think of themselves as friends. They do, however,
spend a great deal of time together, both working in the café
at peak periods and sitting together in Rosy's kitchen when
it is quiet in the café. In the latter circumstance, each is
primarily involved with her own current projects—ironing,
repairing clothes, knitting, reading, cooking and baking—and
there is only minimal conversation between them. Geneviève,
in her capacity as sommelière, is sent on errands to the épicerie
and is expected to interrupt whatever she is doing, even eating

a meal, when someone rings for service in the café downstairs. During the strawberry harvest, she is allowed time off to work in her parents' fields, and, if café business is not too heavy, she may be allowed to leave early to go to a special social event.

Her duties as employee are regular and clearly defined. At the same time, she is a quasi-member of Rosy's ménage— regularly eating at the ménage table, running errands for the household as well as for the café, helping Rosy prepare meals and clean up after them. Rosy knows Geneviève's food preferences and tries to cater to them. Even the act of releasing her from work early to go to a dance is couched in motherly terms. On the other hand, Geneviève often bakes cakes and cookies for Rosy's ménage—working either in her mother's or Rosy's kitchen—and often brings her other small gifts of food, items Rosy is particularly fond of.

The pseudo-ménage relationship is possible because the business relationship is so businesslike: once the terms of work and payment have been settled upon, the employer-employee relationship can be dismissed. Geneviève is then treated as the proprietor's daughter or younger sister who is merely fulfilling her obligations to her ménage by helping in the café. This is, in fact, the situation in the other village café, where a daughter works as sommelière, though with remuneration, of course. Geneviève behaves and is treated as a sort of borrowed daughter of the ménage, and every effort is made on both sides to minimize the actual business relationship—usually through the ménage idiom of food and drink.

The case of Rosy and Geneviève is, perhaps, the perfect example of the extension of the ménage principle to a commercial situation: the ménage metaphor is not exploited only on isolated occasions but is acted out continuously. As a final example, simple but very revealing, I shall consider a commercial relationship which ended dissonantly for both participants because of their conflicting perceptions of the situation. Rosy's café grew out of a small grocery store which she used to operate in the same rooms. On one occasion she needed help in cleaning up the store and called upon an unmarried older woman who lives alone, has no relatives in the village, and is generally considered to be in need financially. The woman agreed to do

the work, but payment was not discussed at the time. When
the job was completed, Rosy asked the woman how much she
should pay her—expecting her to name an amount of money.
The woman would not hear of accepting money and asked only
if she could take some merchandise from the store. Rosy was
puzzled and dissatisfied but finally agreed. "She took just a
few things—some canned meat and a few packages of cookies."
Apparently the two women perceived the job in different ways:
Rosy saw it as a service-payment situation, while the other
woman thought of herself as "helping out" in a neighborly
mutual-aid context. In the first view, the service was extraordinary—that is, not occurring regularly—requiring more time
and effort than a "small service," and, in fact, contracted for
in advance, almost as if it were a professional service. Such
a service establishes a debt on the part of the recipient which
can be dissolved first through a payment of money and then
in the ménage idiom of food and drink. In the second view,
the cleaning-up task was simply a case of "replacement," and
the appropriate payment was in the traditional currency between women of reciprocated labor or produce. The older
woman, with no relatives in the village and in constrained
means, was particularly eager to participate in the "one family"
context—to suppress the business aspect of the relationship and
to enter directly into the ménage mode.

7. Social Gastronomy

Women play the major role in extending the *ménage* principle to social and ritual spheres of behavior, most obviously because this is the behavior that takes place at home, in the private arena. Most of these cases involve actual admission of non-ménage members into the kitchen. These are visiting occasions. The visitors may be friends or neighbors, relatives, or non-villagers of special status such as the parish priest, the insurance salesman, or the anthropologist.

Both social and ritual visits are characterized by conventionalized behavior which expresses both an explicit purpose and an implicit message. These visits can be distinguished in several ways. Social visits are casual and may occur at any convenient time with a minimum of prearrangement; typically, they take place in the context of interpersonal relationships. Ritual visits are formal and occur on specific occasions associated with religious or traditional events; the visitors are usually institutionalized groups, or individuals representing such groups. The existence of social visiting is generally known, but it is private information as to who visits whom, when and for how long, for what reasons, and with what results. On ritual occasions, however—since the visits follow certain public events and the visitors are often non-villagers—the fact and personnel of such visits are known generally.

It is almost impossible to pay a call on a woman without being offered something to drink—usually tea, but occasionally "*une petite liqueur*" or coffee. The ostensible reason for the visit may be delivery of requested goods or information, or solicitation of a small service. Social visiting is a winter activity and constitutes one of the major sources of recreation for women during this slow time of year. Visiting is normally an afternoon event, taking place at any time after the noontime household chores are done—"*après la vaisselle*," at about 1:30 or 2:00—and before it is time to begin the evening milking and stable chores, at about 4:30. During this afternoon period, women are free to engage in special activities—knitting, sewing, repairing clothes, ironing, looking at magazines or seed catalogs, and visiting. Since the daily schedule and its activities are essentially the same for all women and the free afternoon period clearly circumscribed, the time or duration of a visit is not a significant issue. A visit usually lasts for as long as it takes to consume one pot of tea—the time depending on the proportion of chatting to drinking and thus subject to much variation. No matter when a visit begins, however, the visitor would no more think of remaining past 4:30 than she would of arriving at 10 in the morning.

The visitor seeks entrance by knocking at the appropriate door—usually the inner of two front entrances, sometimes the kitchen door itself. The visitor is admitted into the hallway and immediately states her purpose. The two women conduct their business, still standing in the hallway, and then begin to chat about other things. After a few minutes, the hostess offers tea, and the visitor expresses eagerness to leave. When the tea is finally accepted, as it usually is, the two women enter the kitchen. The visitor still expresses reluctance to stay, saying "I didn't come for the tea," and the hostess busies herself preparing the snack—boiling water, bringing out a teapot and cups and her tin box of assorted cookies. The relationship between the two women—how intimately they know each other and how frequently they visit—may determine the choice of teapot, the presence or absence of saucers, and the decision to offer the current box of cookies (which is a collection representing various qualities and ages) or to open a fresh package of cookies or even a packaged cake. A less intimate relationship prescribes the use of a better teapot and of saucers, and the serving of fresh cookies or cake—that is, more elegant and formal service and higher quality food. Again, if the visitor is regarded as more important or less intimately known, the hostess presents the refreshments with initial apologies, both for their quality and for the mode of presentation. The two women resume their conversation about village events and persons or about their own current personal problems. The hostess frequently urges more tea on her guest—*"sers-toi"*—and the visitor refuses a certain number of these urgings—*"merci, ça va très bien."* As the visit draws to a close, reference is made once again to the reason for it. The women move out into the hallway, discussing their business again, and they finally part, thanking each other profusely.

What I have described here is a highly conventionalized social interaction. It illustrates certain key aspects of Brusonin ideology: the perception of privacy and the striving for balanced interpersonal relationships. The visit is justified on the basis of the goods or information exchanged; the exchange is potentially public knowledge, and most of it takes place in the more public part of the house—the hallway. The specific content of this exchange may be private, or very inconsequential, but the essential thing is that there was a specific reason for the visit. Whether the visitor comes as suppliant or as donor of goods or information, she is intruding on the privacy of the hostess' ménage. She knows that, having set foot inside the house, she will be offered food and drink; the hostess will symbolically open the ménage to her. Since such an act is usually associated with payment for services rendered, the social visit is recast in economic terms. The occasion becomes one involving the creation and dissolution of debt toward the smooth functioning of the "one family" that is the village. The inviolateness of the ménage is reaffirmed, and its identifying feature of gastronomic exclusivity is manipulated in the debt-payment context. The one who offers ménage hospitality ultimately has the upper hand. Thus, in order to remain debt-free and on equal footing, the visitor makes clear that she has not come "for the tea." She clearly and lengthily states her purpose and expresses as much disinterest as possible in the refreshments without offending her hostess.

Economic exchanges of time, labor, and produce occur freely between women, without the trappings of elaborate service-payment rituals that take place between men. Social visiting, however, encroaches directly on ménage territory. Women are often seen stopping to chat in the street and even stepping off the street and behind a house or barn as a gesture of privacy upon which passersby will not intrude. But these "visits," occurring visibly in public locations, present no threat to the individual's independence and equality. Hence, no justification or ritualization is necessary, as it is in the case of kitchen visiting. On the street or in the fields, a woman is an individual agent and does not represent her ménage. This is in marked contrast to men's behavior, as I have shown. Men, who are rarely present in the ménage quarters and are associated with it only formally, must carry their ménages around with them, so to speak, and project them larger-than-life on the public field.

When the rules of social visiting are not observed, the visit has a very different meaning. Either the visitor is not a member of the culture, as in the case of the anthropologist, or she is in a dependence relationship with the hostess—both situations being extremely rare in Bruson. In my status as resident outsider, I presented no threat to the standing of any Bruson woman in her village relationships. Although I was regarded as a special case and as being outside the village social system, my visits usually followed the standard pattern. I arrived—sometimes by prearrangement—stated my purpose, conducted my business with the hostess, and then participated with her in the tea ritual of alternate urgings and refusals. Those women with whom I was less intimate treated me accordingly, offering higher-quality refreshments and serving more elegantly and apologetically.

My position was peculiar, however, since most of my visits were not returned—perhaps because most of these women could not conceive of a specific reason with which to visit me. Those few who did visit always did so at my express invitation and for the specific purpose of working with me as informants. Occasionally, a woman stopped by to offer me a gift of garden produce but refused to accept my invitation to have tea, probably because she correctly assessed that any social relationship between us would be inherently unbalanced, and, therefore, she would have nothing to do with it. A few women, exploiting the fact that I was an outsider, freely and informally invited me to visit—"Come and see me"—in open dismissal of the requirement of specific purpose.

Since a dependent relationship is abhorrent to a Brusonin, one can profitably examine one, in this context of social visits as extensions of the ménage principle. Marguerite is visited almost daily by her octogenarian cousin Céline. Céline has never married and lives by herself, across the street from Marguerite. The two women are self-acknowledged "cousins"—Céline is Marguerite's mother's first cousin—and Marguerite can, with difficulty, explain the precise relationship. Céline's visits are tenuously based on this kinship relationship and on the factor of residential proximity, but otherwise the two women have nothing in common. They are about twenty years apart in age, and the conversation they muster between them takes place at two different volume levels, since Céline is almost completely deaf. Céline arrives, with no pretense of purpose, seats herself in her accustomed chair, and watches Marguerite continuing whatever she was doing before—cleaning house or sewing, for instance. If Marguerite is entertaining one or more visitors, Céline simply joins the group. Marguerite regards her cousin as a pathetic indigent—needy of social contact rather than of material goods. She considers her own behavior as charity, given without resentment. She, in turn, never visits Céline. This is clearly a relationship of one-sided dependence which no amount of conventionalized effort can possibly correct. This is a social visit which breaks all the rules of social visiting: there is no explicit purpose, the guest is not invited to the ménage table, and the implicit message is dependence.

In most cases of social visiting, there are only two participants—both of them villagers, relatives, intimately acquainted, and frequent visitors in each other's kitchens. As the size or composition of the group changes, the conventional procedures of a social visit are modified. The explicit purpose may be less well-defined, or expressed later in the course of the visit. The

implicit message of the visit, revealed primarily in the refresh-
ment ritual, will depend entirely on the particular circumstances.

When a new baby is born, and mother and child have
returned from the hospital, it is customary for relatives, quartier neighbors, and other acquaintances to visit the house. The
expressed purpose of the visit, for all the visitors, is "to see
the baby" (*voir le bébé*). They arrive individually and bring
gifts for the baby. At any moment, there may be up to half
a dozen guests, usually seated in the living room. The mother
takes them into the baby's room, one or two at a time, and
the visitors admire the baby, his crib, blanket, and other
furnishings. Meanwhile, the women who have just arrived, or
who have already "seen the baby," remain in the living room,
chatting and examining those gifts which the mother has
already opened. It is unlikely that tea will be served, but the
mother informally offers gift chocolates or cookies to her guests,
and they help themselves freely. It is acknowledged that she
does not yet have the strength to entertain visitors in the
customary way—especially in view of the larger-than-custom-
ary number of visitors. Late in the afternoon, when the group
has diminished to two or three, she may offer to serve tea.
The tea ceremony will be honored—the urgings of the hostess,
her apologies, the guests' refusals—but in a very simple and
relaxed fashion, almost as if out of habit. This relaxation is
due, in part, to allowances made in favor of the new mother's
strength, and also to the fact that these remaining visitors are
on intimate terms with her. The visitors, having satisfied the
requirement of purpose—"to see the baby"—now move into the
social part of the visit, drinking tea and chatting.

With the larger group of women present, the visit is treated
as a public event: the conversation is general among the women,
and none but the most innocuous and impersonal topics are
discussed. This is somewhat surprising when one realizes that
the visitors represent not a random collection of village women
but rather a selection of those who consider themselves on
more friendly terms with the new mother. The explanation
lies in the fact that a Bruson woman has a unique relationship
with each of her fellow Brusonins and functions most comfortably in a one-to-one interaction. Her relationships may be

arranged along a continuum of intimacy, with an underpinning of obligation. The more intimate relationships are those based on longer-standing and more frequent service-payment events. Such relationships are more stable because both women have learned through time and experience that they can count on each other, thus avoiding the possibility of being indebted. A woman may engage in a number of such relationships, but each one, because of its particular history and content, is different. And, of course, it is not necessary that any two of her intimates be intimate with each other.

Thus, the group of women visiting to see the new baby have only one thing in common—they are all on more or less intimate terms with the mother. Otherwise, it is a bizarre collection, including pairs of women who are very close friends or relatives and others who never see each other except on such public occasions. All of them are intruding on the mother's ménage, but—because of the size of the group—there is no opportunity for each individual to behave as is most appropriate in the light of her particular relationship with the mother. Hence, there is a temporary suspension of the rules and conventions governing two-person social visits, and the event is treated as if it were taking place in the public arena of street or fields.

Such group visits are rare and, in fact, usually occur quite by accident. A group tea party generally arises as a result of the serial arrival of individual women, each of whom expects to observe the rules and participate in the rituals of a social visit. These rules and rituals, however, are incompatible with a group visit, since they refer to two-person interactions. One of the consequences is a reversal of what are normally considered the more public and more private part of the house. The new arrival, upon realizing that there are already visitors in the kitchen—thus rendering it the public part of the house— states her purpose in the hallway, out of earshot of the others. This conversation, brief and *sotto voce*, is private in content but public in function, from the point of view of the earlier visitors. That is, it is read as the arrival of an additional potential visitor who is presently fulfilling the requirement of purpose for her visit.

The new arrival will be invited by the hostess to have tea. She peeks into the kitchen, greeting the others and apologizing for the interruption. Whether or not she decides to stay depends on the number of visitors already present and their relationships to the hostess. If only one woman has arrived before her, the new visitor is less likely to remain—especially if her relationship with the hostess is not as intimate as that of the earlier arrival. If, however, there are several women having tea, she recognizes this as a public event during which her relationships with any of these women, the hostess included, will not be activated. She risks nothing in accepting the ménage hospitality, because the very size of the group neutralizes all the paired relationships within it, offering a kind of group anonymity to each individual.

Such group social visits are merely special cases of the standard two-person visit. They require an explicit statement of specific purpose—whether it be the same publicly-related purpose for all visitors, as in the case of a new-baby visit, or an individual privately-stated purpose for each new arrival at a tea party. The implicit message of the group visit is a general agreement to suppress individual interests in favor of group solidarity. The group envisaged in this agreement is not the particular set of women present but the "one family" of the village as a whole, of which these women are a representative segment. Whereas, in the two-person encounter, the debt-free nature of the relationship must be ritually reaffirmed on the occasion of each visit, the group visit assumes individual equality and interpersonal harmony, and the group conducts itself on an impersonal public level. Such an assumption must be made, because the significance and complexity of two-person relationships would otherwise render impossible any group interaction. So, with the appearance of a third visitor, tea is served with a minimum of fuss, and the group settles into the mode of public behavior.

Before leaving the subject of social visits, let us consider a class of events which, though they involve the introduction of non-ménage members into ménage territory, are the antithesis of social visits. I am referring to the movements of people within a converging family. Here, although two separate ménages are involved, the relationship between them permits completely free access, particularly on the part of the female members. Mother and daughter, or daughter-in-law, visit each other frequently, without the necessity of a specific purpose and without observing any of the rituals of social visiting. The kinship or affinal relation is sufficient justification for the visit, and the two women do not regard themselves as guest and hostess. In fact, it is perfectly permissible for a mother to enter a daughter's house in the daughter's absence, and vice versa. Although most such visits are made with a specific purpose, some occur out of a simple and acknowledged desire for companionship—an explicit purpose which is inadmissible in the standard social visit.

A mother brings her daughter some freshly-made jam or requests that her son-in-law drive her to her dental appointment in Martigny. She visits when one of the children is ill and in bed. She baby-sits when her daughter must leave the house. Similarly, the daughter stops in to ask her mother's help in deciphering knitting instructions. She voluntarily does house-cleaning and cooking for her parents when her mother is ill. Both women often work together, baking or sewing, in the kitchen of either one. The daughter may even sleep in her parents' house when her husband must be away overnight. All this applies equally to the relationship between mother and daughter-in-law and, in principle at least, to any relationship within the converging family. In actual practice, the relationship is modified only by factors such as sex—men being generally less active in the house—and degree of intimacy—for instance, the more distant relationship that may exist between a life-long villager and an in-marrying affine.

Even in the presence of others, it is acknowledged that members of the converging family have certain rights. Should a daughter drop in when her mother is having visitors, she will state her purpose, if there is one, openly. She may join the group if she wishes to, but her refusal to remain is stated and accepted without ceremony. If she stays, she helps her mother, as co-hostess, and usually remains to help in the cleaning up. If a mother and daughter are visiting each other, a third person arriving on the scene will not be deterred from staying: the mother and daughter are considered, in a sense, as a single person, so that the visitor does not risk intruding on an intimate relationship between the hostess and the earlier arrival.

What one observes here is not a prescribed violation of

ménage exclusivity but a momentary identification of two ménages as a single one—those two being in the very special relationship of components of a converging family. The free access that characterizes this relationship is a reminder that what are now members of separate and distinct ménages were once members of a single ménage. The technical separation of the ménages of parent and child does not require that the two forego the benefits of acting as one ménage. I have already shown that this converging takes place in the area of food production—a necessity from the point of view both of the children who have no land of their own yet and of the parents who still need their children's labor.

Women form the strongest bonds between the two ménages, since it is they who are most strongly associated with ménage functions. These bonds are intended to include the men, simply by virtue of their being participants in the converging family. Just as in their economic behavior, so also members of the converging family function socially as a single unit. But, whether making spontaneous visits or dining at each other's tables, members of the converging family are not engaging in what I have described as social visits. This special relationship is an extension of the ménage principle but such a perfect extension as to represent an identity of the two units. Converging family members have rights in each other's ménages—something which cannot be said of any other relationship except at the risk of implying social bankruptcy in the village.

8. Ritual Gastronomy

The extension of the *ménage* principle is perhaps most striking in the context of ritual occasions. Whether religious or secular, these occasions are traditional events, occurring at fixed times, and involving group rather than interpersonal contacts. The group may be the village as a whole or a particular segment of it—occupational, recreational, or political. Ritual gastronomy may take place in the form of visiting—actual or symbolic intrusion on ménage privacy—or in the public arena of café or restaurant. In the former case, women are the hostesses, whether acting for their own ménages or as representatives of the village. In the latter case, the group concerned creates a kind of artificial ménage situation, by actually hiring the services and facilities of a public eating and drinking place. These occasions are usually restricted to men, occurring as they do in public.

As in the case of social visiting, ritual gastronomic occasions have an explicit purpose and an implicit message. They differ in that the purpose and message are inherent in the occasion itself and fall in the realm of public knowledge. This is consistent with the Brusonin's conception of individual behavior as private and group behavior as public. Since the ultimate message of a ritual occasion is always group solidarity—whatever group may be specifically referred to—it is also predictable that the vehicle will be an extension of the ménage principle, using the ménage currency of food and drink.

In the private arena, I shall consider three examples of ritual gastronomy, all of which occur in the kitchen (or a symbolic extension thereof) and are thus ritual counterparts of social visits. The first has direct religious significance, the visitor being the priest who comes to the village chapel one morning a week to celebrate the Mass. After the Mass, he is served breakfast in the kitchen of a woman who holds the traditional village office of *procureur*. This woman who "receives the priest" functions for a year, at the end of which time a new procureur is chosen. The choice is made at an annual, village-wide, traditional assembly and is based on year of birth. A slate is presented to the village of all the men born in a particular year, the years being taken sequentially. The villagers vote, and the winner's wife takes on the job of procureur, acting for her husband who, in turn, is acting for the village. The voting is based on such considerations as health, amount of free time, and—most important—whether or not the candidate has a wife or close female relative who can do the job.

This ritual function is so closely associated with the ménage that it is considered a woman's job. If none of the candidates has either a wife or a female relative he can mobilize—a rare occurrence—then the one who is chosen must find and pay some other woman to do the job for him. This payment, incidentally, is not intended primarily to defray the woman's monetary expenses in "receiving the priest" but is rather a customary way of discharging one's social responsibilities indirectly, by hiring another person to function in one's place. Outside the ménage, money is the appropriate payment for services. If, however, there is a woman available within the ménage, she is expected to function without payment, and, in fact, a certain honor is attached to the office of procureur. She is opening her ménage, in the name of the entire village, to an important and high-status visitor. In so doing, she is dissolving the village's debt to the priest for his religious services, denying that there is a commercial relationship, and, finally, putting the village in the morally superordinate position of host.

On other religious occasions women extend ménage hospitality as individuals rather than in an official capacity. Because these are ritual occasions, concerning institutionalized groups, the women are also acting indirectly in the name of that group. One such opportunity arises during the Week of Rogations in the early spring. During this week, the parish priests lead groups of men, women, and children in silent marches around the valley, terminating each time in a different village where the Mass is celebrated. The marching group consists of members of various villages, who are entertained by members of the host village where the Mass is finally sung. Not only are the visitors offered the facilities of the village chapel, but they are also invited individually to join individual ménages at breakfast after the Mass. The invitations are extended informally and spontaneously to visitors who are relatives, affines, or simply friends. These breakfasts are the ritual counterparts of group social visits. Their explicit purpose is the occasion itself—the Rogations march—and the implicit message is to enhance the reputation of the host village—"we Brusonins are known for our hospitality." Thus, although conducted through the medium of the individual ménage, these ritual visits express group solidarity—where the group of reference is the village in whose name the individual members are acting.

The patron-saint's day, dedicated to the Archangel Michael —St. Michel—offers several examples of ritual gastronomy with secular referents. In spite of the religious basis of the occasion, this is really a secular holiday—a fête—and the only one that is village-wide and village-specific. In fact, even the religious basis itself is open to question. The choice of St. Michel as the village patron goes back to the seventeenth century when the present chapel was built, largely with the funds of a villager named Michel Filliez. It seemed appropriate to honor this man by naming his saintly counterpart as the village's spiritual patron. Unfortunately, however, St. Michel's birthday—the usual choice for such a celebration—falls in late September, a very busy time in the agricultural cycle. Instead, the Brusonins chose to celebrate their patron saint on the date of an important event in his life, his battle with the devil—which, happily, fell on May 8, a less occupied time agriculturally and the beginning of "la belle saison."

Once adopted as patron, however, St. Michel began to function in a religious context, in spite of the practical and secular

process of adoption. He became the object of religious supplica-
tion, especially at times of village crisis. A story is related about
how St. Michel once stopped the rushing destructive flow of
a mountain stream before it could reach Bruson. This was done
in response to a specific request on the part of the villagers
and with their promise that, if he did this, they would say
the Rosary in his honor every evening.

There is, however, no reference made to this event of particular village interest or to any other personal characteristic of
St. Michel on the occasion of the *fête patronale*. The priest
who comes to the village to celebrate the Mass may use the
story of St. Michel's battle with the devil as material for his
sermon, but otherwise the figure of the saint is treated as a
general inspirational object. The battle is actually translated
into secular terms by the young unmarried men of the village,
who form the Army of St. Michel—marching in formation
through the village, carrying army rifles and decorated toy
hatchets and sabers, and shooting off blanks at specific times
upon the order of their *Commandant*. This is the traditional
contribution to the fête patronale of *"la Jeunesse"* who are,
in other contexts as well, treated as a distinct group.

Another group that plays a traditional role in the St. Michel
festivities is the men's singing society, called Alpenrose. The
fête patronale is, in fact, one of their big days, an occasion
for public performance of the music they have been rehearsing
all winter. They play a major role in the religious part of the
day, singing the Mass in the village chapel. La Jeunesse—the
Army of St. Michel—also participates in the Mass, shooting a
few volleys of blanks during the Sanctus. Another village
group that participates in the Mass is the pair of teenage girls
who hold the annual office of *prieuses*. Chosen on the basis
of their year of birth, they are specifically responsible for the
daily Rosary dedicated to St. Michel, and, as an extension of
this function, they distribute the traditional sweet bread to
all the celebrants at the end of the Mass. Their position is
slightly different from that of Alpenrose and La Jeunesse in
that the group they represent is the village as a whole, in its
relationship to the patron saint.

At the conclusion of the Mass, at about noon, the Alpenrose
group and the priest pay a ritual visit to the procureur who

serves them wine just outside her house. She is acting in her capacity as the village's representative in religious affairs, and her hospitality is conceived of as payment for religious services. She then "receives the priest" at her dinner table, while the Alpenrose men repair to the café to celebrate their group triumph of the morning.

Eventually, everyone goes home to lunch, a festive and elaborate meal to which are invited various non-villagers—most of them Brusonins who have married out of the village and returned with their families on this important occasion, but also some persons of special status like the non-resident school-teacher or the resident anthropologist. This is the occasion for an annual, or even-less-frequent reunion of relatives and friends. Again, the individual ménage is playing host to the visitors in the name of the entire village upon the occasion of an important, public, traditional event. The visitors, for their part, fall into the general category of returning relatives, affines, or friends. The explicit purpose of these visits is the ritual occasion itself, and the implicit message is, once again, enhancement of the public image of Bruson and a display of village solidarity through the ménage idiom of food and drink.

At about two in the afternoon, the secular part of the day begins. The entire village, led by the Army of St. Michel, pays ritual visits to certain key villagers: the procureur, the two conseillers who represent Bruson on the communal council, the prieuses, and, finally, officials in the Army of St. Michel—the Commandant and the Porte-Drapeau, or flag-bearer. As the group arrives at each house, the Army fires a volley in salute of the host, the host makes a speech, the women of the ménage serve wine all around, and Alpenrose sings a few secular songs.

The host, in each case, represents a village status rather than a particular villager, since the actual personnel changes regularly. The procureur, as religious liaison, introduces the priest who makes the speech. The conseillers represent the village's temporal interests in the larger polity of the commune. They take this opportunity to make "political" speeches—thanking the villagers for their support and referring to their election promises which will contribute to the future and greater glory of the village. At the houses of the prieuses—who also represent "les filles" in general—speeches are dispensed with altogether,

and wine and cigarettes are offered. Those among the villagers
who remain continue on to the houses of the Commandant
and the Porte-Drapeau, where there is a minimum of ceremony,
and, at last, the group returns to the chapel where the Army
formally disbands.

At each stop along this route, the explicit purpose is to honor
the host and to express appreciation for his public activities
on behalf of the village. As if to emphasize his role as public
servant, he is now required to serve the public wine. Having
already been paid for his services—in money, in honor, or
both—he uses this public occasion to re-establish himself as
an equal member of the "one family" of the village by using
the ménage idiom of food and drink. Thus, the wine is, at the
same time, payment for honors received and dissolution of a
moral debt incurred in accepting those honors.

Because these are ritual visits—public, traditional, and involving social groups rather than individuals—their meaning
is quite transparent. Both the conventions and the content
of these visits are clearly stated and universally known. Participants in a social visit are constantly jockeying for position,
with respect to each other, through a series of what are
essentially denial rituals: "I didn't come for the tea," the
apologies of the hostess, and so forth. In these ritual visits
associated with the fête patronale, however, it is explicitly
stated that the hosts must "*donner à boire*"—serve drinks to
the group—that speeches will be made whose content is completely predictable and therefore completely insignificant, and
that Alpenrose and La Jeunesse will perform their prescribed
functions as well as they can under the increasing influence
of the wine which is their payment for performing those
functions.

"*La St. Michel*," this glorious paean to village identity and
unity, ends with a public dance in the village schoolhouse—one
of the rare events in which men, women, and children participate equally. This is the only public occasion when the entire
ménage sits together and interacts socially. The fête patronale,
as the perfect expression of village solidarity, thus grants
recognition to the separate ménages that compose the "one
family."

Purely secular occasions of ritual gastronomy, the men's

domain, are of two kinds: one in which the visiting group is not in any way associated with the village, and another in which the participants represent only a specific village segment rather than the village as a whole. Both of these are public occasions involving intergroup behavior—thus falling in the realm of ritual rather than social gastronomy. They differ only in the degree of public participation. In the first case, the entire village, represented by one individual, plays host to the visiting outsiders. In the second case, only a particular special-interest group within the village is involved, a group which is not generally thought to be representing Bruson as a whole.

During the spring and summer, the Val de Bagnes is often the site of various regional fêtes—festivals of bands, of singing societies, of women's folklore groups. These groups, coming from different villages in nearby communes, assemble in the central square of Le Châble and perform for an audience composed mainly of Bagnards but also of interested persons in the entire region. There is an informal air of competition among them, with respect to their costumes, their marching spirit, and their performance abilities.

At the end of the public concert, each visiting group is put in the hands of a *commissaire*—a man chosen by the commune-wide organizing committee to represent his village as host to the visitors. The choice is made informally, the committee approaching an individual directly and asking if he will serve. Usually, but not necessarily, the individuals approached are those known to have facilities for entertaining a group of visitors—specifically, facilities for serving food and drink. The ideal choice is, of course, the owner of a village café, but the burden cannot always be placed on the same one or two persons. So it often falls on others who must find some way of providing the traditional light supper to the guests, either with the aid of female relatives or by hiring the services of a village café-owner. The committee naturally avoids approaching individuals who are debilitated by age or illness or who are in financial straits. Since, however, it is an honor to be named commissaire, the job is sometimes accepted by older men, retired and living on their pensions, who appreciate the opportunity to be of service to the community.

The commissaire conducts the visiting group—a band, let us

say—to his village where they give a brief performance in some convenient public location, outdoors if the weather is good. In the meantime, the women of the commissaire's ménage are busy preparing a traditional (and relatively inexpensive) cold supper—wine and an *"assiette,"* or plate of dried meat slices, cheese, pickles, and bread. Again, weather permitting, tables are set up outdoors, and the visitors sit down with the commissaire to eat and drink, quite oblivious to the stares of curious village children who gather around to watch.

The occasion has cost the commissaire perhaps one hundred francs—approximately equivalent to two days' work as an *ouvrier*, or a day's intake at the café. This sum is not considered exorbitant or unjust—except when the same person is burdened with it several times within a short period—and the rewards, though of temporary duration, are valuable. The village is opening its collective ménage to an outside group through the person of the commissaire, who actually assumes the labor and cost of hospitality. Food and drink are offered as payment for pleasure received. Thus, the transaction is symbolically removed from the commercial sphere, and the village once again expresses its unity and displays its identifying feature of warm hospitality to the outside world.

The traditional light supper—the *souper*—is the vehicle for a second version of ritual gastronomy in the public arena, this one involving only particular special-interest groups rather than the village as a whole. The souper is given in the name of that group, whether it be an occupational group—the employees of a business enterprise—or a voluntary association such as the village singing society. The Brusonins may form only part of the entire group, or they may constitute the entire group if it is village-specific. The occasion of the souper is usually expressed in temporal terms—*"le souper de la fin d'année"*—and is very much standardized with respect to all such groups within the valley. It is an annual event, falling during the Christmas-New Year's holiday season; it is held in a public restaurant or café in Le Châble, with a traditional menu of either an *assiette* or *raclette* (melted cheese served with boiled potatoes and pickles); it is restricted to actual members of the group, excluding their relatives or friends; and it expresses the unity of the group with respect to the outside world.

By sitting down to a meal together, the group simulates the ménage situation and spirit. It claims for itself—and announces to the world—the solidarity and exclusivity of the ménage. On this occasion, the group is supreme. It rigidly excludes outsiders from the event, and, to celebrate its supremacy, it sanctions and even encourages the violation of certain rules and usages. Thus, men eat and drink outside their ménages, return home late and drunk, and are not liable to the usual reproach or abuse from their neglected wives. If they return home unusually late or exceptionally drunk, they are subjected to good-humored teasing for several days afterward. This prescribed abandonment of one's own ménage is regarded as a man's right and duty in his capacity as member of a special-interest group. On this infrequent but regular occasion, the group claims his entire loyalty.

When the group concerned is a business enterprise, the event carries an additional message. In this case, the souper is given by the entrepreneur for his employees. His ostensible motive is to express thanks for their year-long loyalty to the enterprise. Since they have already been paid for their professional services in the proper monetary currency of the economic sphere, the souper takes on the function of denying the commercial relationship between employer and employee. This situation, on the scale of the valley, is comparable to the village situation in which a professional service is rendered and paid for, and the two men then go off to "have a drink." Again, in the souper of the business enterprise, the employer is minimizing the business relationship and transferring it into the "one family" sphere of mutual aid—thereby encouraging his workers to continued loyalty, for which he is thanking them.

Since essentially all the special-interest groups in the valley consist of male membership, these occasions of ritual gastronomy occur in public places where women are usually not seen except when accompanied by their husbands. There are, however, two such groups whose membership includes both men and women. These are the cooperative health insurance societies which are valley-wide and associated traditionally with each of the two major political parties. Even when women did not vote, they had political affiliation which they inherited from their fathers. Therefore, they were entitled to be present on these occasions of ritual gastronomy.

It is probably the presence of women which brings about the substitution, for the standard souper, of a *dîner*—an elaborate midday meal much like the holiday dinner in the ménage. The women's presence, as well as the greater size of this group, also lends a certain formality to the occasion, in the form of more careful dress and extensive speech-making. These are only minor variations, however, and the essential function of the event—the expression of group solidarity through the ménage medium of food and drink—is retained. Also retained is the sanctioned breaking of certain rules on the part of the individual in favor of the group. Thus, a woman—who normally does not appear in cafés or restaurants, particularly if she is not with her husband—is expected to participate in this event even in her husband's absence. This is a frequent occurrence, since there are many "mixed marriages," with respect to political affiliation, and since the membership of these health insurance societies is limited by political party. Thus, in the context of ritual gastronomy, even a woman may violate social rules in favor of the supremacy of the special-interest group of which she is a member.

In my examination of ritual gastronomy in the public arena, I have moved from the level of ménage and village to that of the valley as a whole, where special-purpose groups employ the ménage principle to simulate the solidarity and exclusivity of the ménage. I have also observed a blurring of sexual distinctions with respect to participation in such events. One can now affirm that the ménage idiom of food and drink is an important unifying device at several cultural levels and for both sexes.

Part III

Family, Friends,
and Associates

9. Social Relations in Bruson

"Here you don't need friends, because you have a very extensive family, on both sides." The speaker is Jeanne, a married woman of fifty-three, who has seven children—a married daughter with a child who lives in Geneva, a married son who lives in another village in the valley, an unmarried daughter who has lived in New York City for about six years, two unmarried daughters and an unmarried son who all work in Geneva but come to Bruson every weekend, and a thirteen-year-old son who lives at home and goes to the Collège in Le Châble. Jeanne, whose mother came from another village, has no close relatives in Bruson. Her unmarried sister and her married brother live elsewhere but maintain their dead father's house in the village and visit very often, as do Jeanne's married children. Jeanne engages in an active friendship with the *ménage* living next door to her father's house in a different *quartier* from her own. She says—"our families have always been friends"—and she believes it very likely that they are distantly related. She claims distant and unspecifiable kinship ties with several others in the village. The woman she finally names as a "best friend" is the daughter of her husband's first cousin.

In sharp contrast, Jeanne's husband, Louis, has the following relatives living in Bruson: two sisters, two nieces and two nephews, one grand-niece, an uncle and an aunt, seven first cousins, seventeen descending first cousins "once-removed" (that is, first cousins' children), four ascending first cousins "once-removed" (that is, first cousins of his parents), and fourteen second cousins and their forty children. Louis can claim and specify kinship—five generations in depth, both lineally and collaterally—with eighty-nine other Brusonins. If one adds to this figure his wife and the four children who live at least some of the time in the village, this brings his kinship network to a total of ninety-four persons, or almost 40 percent of the entire village population. His "best friend" is a non-kins-man age-mate.

While Louis has an unusually large kinship network, Jeanne is one of the very few Brusonins who has no close collaterals living in the village. This makes her statement about friends and family even more interesting, since she refers specifically to "extensive family, on both sides." Apparently, she perceives her husband's relatives as being, in some way, her own and, thus, sees herself as being equally embedded in an extensive kinship network. As for the friends "you don't need," Jeanne and Louis affirm—"you have friends everywhere."

These remarks were made during the course of one of six in-depth interviews I conducted with the object of learning something about the definition and nature of "close relatives" (*proches parents*) and the place of friendship and other associations in Bruson. The interviews were informal and involved the participation of as many members of a single ménage as could be found, ranging from one to four. In one case, the interviewees were members of a converging family—a mother and her married daughter. The interviews began with a general discussion of quartiers—their names, their boundaries, and any features of interest that distinguished them. This was followed by two crucial questions: "Where do your close relatives live?" and "Where do your best friends [*meilleurs amis*] live?" My informants had no difficulty with the first question, although some of them hesitated to include parents and children in the category "close relatives." This is consistent with my previous discussion of the special nature of the converging family—two ménages linked lineally, whose members were once members of a single ménage. There was little hesitation, however, at naming siblings who lived in separate ménages as "close relatives," and none at all with respect to "aunts" and "uncles" (parents' siblings) and a general category of "cousins."

The second question—"Where do your best friends live?"— evoked similar responses from all informants. The first reaction was one expressing lack of comprehension of the term "best friends." This was followed by chuckles of embarrassment and amusement. "One doesn't, after all, have *enemies*," said an informant jokingly, implying that one cannot, therefore, be said to have friends. "It's not like in the city," she continued. "Here everyone hangs around together [*se côtoie*] more or less." Another informant put it this way: "Everyone in this village is acquainted [*se connaît*] to about the same degree."

These responses stood in sharp contrast to those elicited from a group of twenty-four school children who were asked the identical question: "Where do your best friends live?" Each child replied without the slightest hesitation or confusion—citing not only the quartier of residence but even, in three instances, the name of the "best friend." The negative and apparently evasive responses of the adult groups interviewed were even more surprising, since I had often discussed "best friend" relationships in informal conversation with individual Brusonins. On those occasions, as well as in the case of the school children, my informants spoke freely about "best friends." One informant even suggested a typology of friendship, which I eventually shaped into my analytic model. The typology consisted of named categories, the affective base for each, and the linguistic and behavioral concomitants of each type. The affective definition of "best friends"—"people in whom you confide"—reappeared in the six group interviews, each time suggested by the interviewees themselves. Having stated this definition, they were able to continue the discussion. The following is a particularly interesting fragment from one of these interviews, in direct response to the question: "Where do your best friends [people in whom you confide] live?"

Jean: Mostly in Clou—cousins.
Marguerite (his wife): Those are, after all, our best friends—the
    relatives. But there are friends throughout the village.
Jean: One has contact with—
Marguerite: —with everybody.

Jean: Yes. I admit that your relations with certain people are
a little more intimate, but that's especially so with your
relatives—more or less, let's say, of your own age.

Marguerite: My greatest friend lives in Sarreyer—she's always
been my friend.

Jean: A childhood friend.

Marguerite: Since the age of 13. We're in the same *classe*. We
took First Communion together.

This dialogue reiterates the theme that friendship—if it exists
at all—is merely an aspect of kinship, perhaps even impossible
under other circumstances. Jean makes this statement explicitly. Marguerite emphasizes the point by naming, as her
"best friend," a woman of Sarreyer—that is, someone outside the village sphere. At the same time, she introduces
the idea of *classe*—the group of Bagnards born in the same
year—and implicitly offers this universally recognized non-
kinship association, which originates in childhood, as a justification for friendship.

All these informants expressed a certain reserve and caution
in discussing close friendships. Although each ultimately admitted to having one or more "best friends"—"people in whom
you confide"—they insisted that friendship exists among all
Brusonins. To prove the point, men referred to their work
associates and women to the neighbors whom they see daily
in the quartier. Not only was there this sentiment that "here
we are all friends," but several informants also referred to the
reputation of Brusonins, throughout the region, as being hospitable ("*acceuillants*" or "*hospitaliers*") to outsiders. "The *caves*
are open to all passersby, even to those who are not from here
[*pas de chez nous*]. This is a specialty of the village. In Bruson,
no matter where you go, they'll open the door of the cave for
you and offer you a drink—even for people who come to deliver
merchandise. I've heard this many times."

Bruson, then, is described as a place where friendship exists
among all the people and is even extended to non-Brusonins.
Kinship, too, is thought to be widespread, and the kinship
network is expandable, either through imputation of kinship
ties when they cannot be precisely specified, or through such
mechanisms as marriage when husband and wife assume each
other's kinship networks. Friendship ties are said to be found

most often among kinsmen. But since kinship is widespread
and expandable, then it is quite reasonable for Brusonins to
believe that friendship is general among them.

What is not reasonable in these terms and, therefore, requires
explanation is the extension of friendship, in the form of
hospitality, to non-Brusonins, and the existence of "best
friends" who are not necessarily kinsmen. These are events
outside the kinship-friendship system that Brusonins describe.
The first of these—hospitality to strangers—is readily and
proudly admitted. The second—the existence of "best friends"—
although part of the experience of many Brusonins, is reluctantly admitted and accompanied by explanation of the circumstances of each relationship. A "best friend" relationship,
for instance, may have originated in childhood; or it is
associated with the work situation, or with one of the special-
purpose groups such as a political party; or its exists with a
non-villager.

While hospitality to strangers can easily be understood as
an extension of the quartier or work-group friendships, which
require no special explanation and no great commitment, the
"best friend" relationships seem to contradict the basic syllo-
gism and its conclusion: kinship is broad and expandable;
friendship usually occurs within the kinship network; therefore,
here we are all friends. The fact is that "best friend" relationships *are* special, not general throughout the village, and they
depend on the circumstances and decisions of individuals. The
sentiment—"here we are all friends"—does not mean or imply
that "here we are all *best* friends." This would be impossible,
by definition. Rather, what is implied is that "here we are all
friendly—towards each other and even towards outsiders." A
distinction is made between friendliness and friendship, between acquaintance and confidence, between those persons
with whom you "hang around together" (any villagers) and
those persons "in whom you confide" (best friends).

These two forms of affective association may also be described, using Wolf's terminology (1966), as "instrumental
friendship" and "emotional friendship." The first is a system
of mutual-aid relationships, open to all villagers by virtue of
their actual, potential, or imputed kinship ties. It is not a linear
arrangement of points, but rather a general network which any

individual may enter anywhere and at any time. Its affective base is "friendliness," and it is institutionalized in the sense that the system survives any particular individual participant.

Emotional friendship occurs in Bruson in the form of "best friend" relationships. Each of these relationships is unique in origin, participants, and activities—all these factors depending on the individuals involved. Since the affective base is confidence, such a relationship is implicitly closed. For the same reason, the number of such relationships that an individual may have is limited. The individual who "confides in" many people is simply said to be a *mauvaise langue*—not a "best friend" but a malicious gossip. Emotional friendship, being a closed and individually-determined relationship, is dissociated from the village social structure and stands outside the kinship-friendship system. It is not, like kinship, a basic and inescapable attribute of every Brusonin. In fact, as I have noted before, emotional friendship represents a contradiction of the village social system, since it may—and often does—exist outside the bounds of kinship and even of the village itself.

While kinship ties are typically village-wide and instrumental in nature—forms of "friendliness"—friendship ties are usually of the emotional type and limited by individual choice and to individual participation. Brusonins also have a third possibility for association with others, this one in the context of special-purpose groups—economic, religious, political, or recreational—which may be limited to village membership or may be valley-wide. What brings such a group together is neither kinship nor friendship, although both may exist in the group, but rather a specific interest and goal that its members share—cooperative marketing of strawberries, for instance, or adherence to the tenets of a political party, or a love of music. Although individual needs may be satisfied by such a group, the group is formed for the achievement of some common objective. It is, therefore, not a mutual-aid network based on reciprocity and instrumental friendship, nor is it an expression of strong affective ties such as are found in emotional friendship. Although many of these special-purpose groups are now institutionalized, they are all, in principle at least, mutable and even dissolvable, should their objective be achieved.

Kinship is inescapable, friendship is optional, and special-purpose association is expedient. Kinship and special-purpose association have in common their transcendence of the individual. Neither depends on the participation of any particular individual, and both are governed by virtue of the individual's agreement to suppress his personal interests in favor of the group. The individual gives up some of his freedom in order to participate. The essential difference between these two kinds of association lies in the factor of choice: an individual cannot choose his kinship network, although he can expand it or ignore it—both at some personal cost; an individual can, however, choose a particular special-purpose group—always at the expense of some personal freedom—or he has the option of choosing none at all. In either case—kinship or special-purpose association—the individual is subject to group regulation. The only regulation governing friendship, however, is mutual respect of confidence, and this may be interpreted in a variety of ways, depending on the individual participants to the relationship.

While the nature and conduct of a friendship are individually determined and regulated, its existence and its participants are influenced by factors outside the relationship. The same is true of the kinship network, although here the outside influences act not on its existence but on its breadth. In each particular case, the actual extent of one's kinship network and the existence of emotional friendships, within or outside of it, depend on such variables as age, place of origin, marital status, and opportunities for extra-village associations. Thus, for example, a man of seventy-five may have a very small kinship network simply because he has outlived most of his relatives. A woman coming from outside Bruson may have no relatives of her own in the village, lineal or collateral, but may have a large group of "adopted" collaterals through her husband—who may himself have been forced to marry outside Bruson because of his large kinship network which limited his choice of spouse locally. A five-year-old child may have few cousins because his parents' siblings are still too young to have married. At the age of fourteen, the same child may have a "best friend"—perhaps an unrelated age-mate, or a cousin. At eighteen, having left the confines of the village to take up an apprenticeship, he may have formed an emotional friendship with a fellow apprentice from another village.

Upon marriage he acquires an additional set of kinsmen, those of his wife. At the same time that his instrumental friendship network is expanded, there is a tendency toward contraction within the sphere of emotional friendship. Marriage has an isolating effect on both partners and makes it difficult to maintain any but the closest emotional friendships. It represents great responsibility, especially when children begin to arrive, and there is a concomitant loss of personal freedom. Since personal freedom is maximal in emotional friendship, it is this area of association that suffers most. At the same time, however, the responsibilities of marriage implicitly include more active participation in special-purpose groups. The relatively free choice of group enables the individual to recover some of his lost freedom, the freedom that is associated with childhood and youth and expressed in emotional friendships. With his kinship network ever present and now expanded, he has exchanged the friendship of childhood for the expedience of maturity.

In this Part, I will explore these three facets of social relations in Bruson: kinship, friendship, and voluntary association. First I will describe the kinship network, working from its specific contemporary manifestation in the household back to its diffuse and distant origins in the set of village founders. Using this structural framework, I will examine inheritance, from the point of view both of an individual and of the village as a unit. To conclude the section on kinship, I will study the relationship between an individual and his kin network in ideological terms. Then I will focus on friendship in its various forms and functions, and, finally, will examine special-purpose groups as another kind of association available to Brusonins.

10. Family and Famille

The kinship network in Bruson may be viewed as a wheel whose hub is the *ménage*. This unit, created by the marriage of two individuals, generates two additional social groups: the converging family, consisting of the *ménage* itself and the families of orientation of husband and wife, and the *parents*, or collaterals and married siblings of husband and wife. Taken together, these two groups—the converging family and the *parents*—form the *parenté* of that particular ménage. But the ménage also has historical meaning and continuity, its family name being passed down through the generations. It is part of a patrinomial descent group called a *famille*, whose origins are placed in the distant past among a generalized group of village founders, the *ancêtres*. (See Figure 2.) The wheel of kinship and its history will form the conceptual framework for this discussion.

A Brusonin uses the term *la parenté* to refer collectively to all his living relatives, whether or not presently residing in the village. If he is married, the term also embraces his wife's relatives, although he uses special terms to set apart particular persons as affines rather than as "adopted" consanguineal relatives. These persons are his wife's lineal relatives: *belle-mère, beau-père, belle-soeur, beau-frère*, and—with no special term available—*grandmère de ma femme*, and *grandpère de ma femme*. "*La parenté*," then, may be translated as "family," in the American English usage—that is, all of one's living relatives, consanguineal or affinal (Schneider:1968). The American term "*the* family," or "the immediate family"—a residential unit—is referred to in Bruson as "*le ménage*," which is usually a nuclear family (or the remnants of one) and occasionally an extended family. The context of ménage is the occasion for one of the very rare uses of the word famille in Bruson: *père de famille*, denoting a man who is married and has children. Here, "*famille*" is used in the same way as "family" in the English sentence: "Do you have any family?" (that is, "Do you have children?").

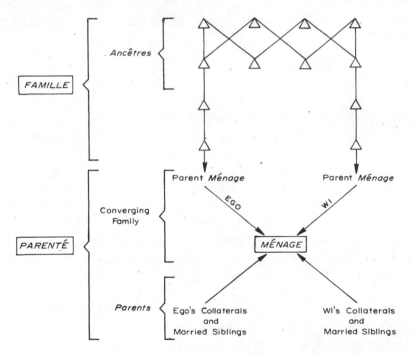

Figure 2. *Ménage, Parenté*, and *Famille*.

Although the ménage is part of the parenté, its members are not considered *parents* (relatives). This term refers to the non-residential segment of the parenté: collaterals, wife's collaterals, siblings, and wife's siblings who reside in their own ménages. Lineals other than siblings are not thought of as *parents*. These persons are members of the converging family which, like the ménage, stands in a special relationship to a Brusonin.

Parents may be specified as being "*du côté de ma mère (mon père)*"—"on my mother's (father's) side"—and usually refer to relatives in the two ascending generations. Beyond *grandparents* there is a nebulous semi-mythical region of distant lineals. One does not usually have a living great-grandparent—*arrière grandparent*—except in earliest childhood, and he is easily forgotten thereafter as a real person. He is most often called *ailleul* and, thus, removed terminologically from the line of descent. Although some people can, if pressed, name lineals whose terms are preceded by one or more arrière, for most Brusonins this distant region of kinship is that of les ancêtres. Les ancêtres are not only one's own distant lineal ascendants but also a generalized group of village founding fathers. They are the almost legendary Brusonins who kept cows and grew cereals, forage, and grapes; who baked bread twice a year in communal ovens; who were confined to their village through the long, hard winter; who produced large families and lived on the products of their land and labor. The ancêtres were hardy people of good peasant stock. Although the modern Brusonin aspires to owning a washing machine and having central heating in his house, he reveres the ancêtres and their heritage.

Les parents, then, are all relatives and affines who are not members of the ménage or the converging family: married siblings, collaterals, and by expansion, wife's married siblings and wife's collaterals. The wife's lineal relatives, with the exception of her married siblings, are members of the converging family and, thus, are not considered *parents*. Since the group of *parents* includes some of the husband's relatives and some of the wife's relatives, it is unique to each ménage—except in the infrequent but known event of two sisters marrying two brothers, in which case both ménages have the same set of *parents*. Unmarried siblings, of course, have identical *parents*.

The parenté of a Brusonin thus consists of his *parents* (including those of his wife), his ménage, and the two converging family units of which he is a member. Like the group of *parents*, the parenté is unique to each ménage. In both cases, the ménage is regarded as a single individual and represented, on most

occasions, by any member thereof, since all members share a
parenté. Only upon marriage and the creation of a new ménage
does a new parenté come into existence.

Les ancêtres, as long-dead antecedents, are a group apart
from the parenté. Sometimes they and their living descendants
are referred to specifically by family names. This is another
of the rare occasions when the word famille is used. It refers
to all the people bearing the same family name, now or in
the past, who are presumed to be related, more or less distantly.
Positive or neutral attributes are ascribed to each famille. Thus,
one speaks of the Fellays as a famille de Bagnes of the same
original stock as the Filliezs; of the Gards who came to Bagnes
from the Val d'Aosta in the fourteenth century; of the Bailli-
fards whose famille is one of the largest today; of the Marets
of Bruson as opposed to the Marets of Lourtier—"*c'est un autre
'Maret'* " ("that's a different 'Maret' "); of the Roserens who
are all Radicals politically; of the Deslarzes whose name comes
from the patois word for "larch"; of the four Besse babies born
in the village one year (all bearing the name Besse but not
known to be related).

The concept of famille falls in the realm of Brusonin cosmology which, in this respect, is very reminiscent of the Australian
aboriginal "dreaming." The famille is, strictly speaking, outside
the limits of kinship. It is a timeless unit. In the very distant
past it was part of the group of ancêtres—both one's own
ancestors and, by extension, the common ancestors of all
Brusonins, the village founders. The descendants of these
original familles continue to exist into the present, in a kind
of existence that parallels but is not part of actual parenté.
Just as the ancêtres founded Bruson and supplied a tradition
and heritage for the village, so their descendants, the familles,
represent the present and continuing unity of the village as
a cultural entity.

This cosmological system is supported and confirmed by
actual demographic data. A study of family names found in
the village today and a comparison of these with names present
in 1910 reveals some remarkable facts. First of all, there is a
stable group of fourteen family names present both in 1910
and 1969. Although the population has been drastically reduced
in these fifty-nine years—from 423 to 250—these fourteen family

names encompass 82 percent (1910) and 85 percent (1969) of all resident Brusonins. Even more striking is the fact that six of these family names account for two-thirds of the population—the *same* six names in both censuses. Since the total number of family names in each case is twenty-six (1910) and twenty-four (1969), two-thirds of the people bear one-quarter of the names. (See Tables 1 and 2.)

Of the twelve names of highest frequency in the population of 1910, ten have remained in the same group in 1969, and the other two have become extinct. Unfortunately, I did not have information on citizenship and origin for the 1910 family names. In 1969, on the other hand, all non-*bourgeois* or non-Brusonin names are in the group of lowest frequency in the

TABLE 1

FAMILY NAMES: 1969

	Percent of Population (N=250)	Name	Present in 1910	Brusonin	Percent of Names (N=24)
66	16	Besse	X	X	25
	14	Maret	X	X	
	10	Vaudan	X	X	
	10	Baillifard	X	X	
	8	Bruchez	X	X	
	8	Filliez	X	X	
22	5	Roserens	X	X	25
	5	Allaman			
	4	Deslarzes	X	X	
	3	Alter	X	X	
	3	Gard	X	X	
	2	Genoud	X	X	
12	2	Rozain		X	50
	2	Latapie			
	2	Burcher			
	<1	Bessard	X	X	
	<1	Besson	X	X	
	<1	Fellay			
	<1	Stoller			
	<1	Theodoloz			
	<1	Nicollier	X	X	
	<1	Masson			
	<1	Pitteloud			
	<1	Thetaz			

TABLE 2

FAMILY NAMES: 1910[a]

Percent of Population (N=423)	Name	Present in 1969	Percent of Names (N=26)
16	Maret	X	
16	Filliez	X	
14	Vaudan	X	
66 7	Baillifard	X	25
7	Bruchez	X	
6	Besse	X	
4	Deslarzes	X	
4	Morand		
3	Carron		
17 2	Roserens	X	25
2	Alter	X	
2	Genoud	X	
2	Nicollier	X	
2	Besson	X	
2	Guigoz		
<1	Gard	X	
<1	Bessard	X	
<1	Deurin		
<1	Pache		
17 <1	Gailland		50
<1	Luisier		
<1	May		
<1	Moulin		
<1	Roduit		
<1	Rossier		
<1	Gabbud		

[a] Information on origin not available.

population, representing 2 percent or fewer of all Brusonins. The one exception, Allaman, accounts for 5 percent of the population but exists as a single ménage—the largest one in the village, consisting of parents and their nine resident children.

The top six names in both censuses represent not only two-thirds of the total population on both dates but also—in 1969 only, since I lack the comparable data for 1910—two-thirds of the total number of ménages (forty-nine out of seventy-five), two-thirds of all marriages (forty out of fifty-eight), two-thirds of all unmarried individuals over twenty years of age (forty out of sixty-four), and a little more than two-thirds of all individuals under twenty (fifty out of seventy). These data strongly justify my referring to these six names as those of "core familles" and presenting them as evidence both for actual demographic continuity and for the Brusonin cosmology of familles.

The famille is a genetic, social, and historical concept to the Brusonin. The genetic concept is revealed with reference to marriage. Because all living members of a famille—that is, all bearers of the family name—are believed to be more or less distantly related, the familles tend to be exogamous. Of the forty-four married women born after 1900 and living in Bruson today, only one has the same maiden and married names—rather than the four predicted by a simple mathematical model. And, in fact, this one case is, in a sense, accidental, since the husband's father was an illegitimate child. Had he been born in wedlock, it is very unlikely that he would have carried the family name in question. As an illegitimate child, however, he took his mother's maiden name. The contemporary married couple are actually direct lineal descendants of two brothers who lived in the early nineteenth century. Although third cousins once-removed, they claim they are not related: *"C'est un autre Vaudan."* ("It's a different Vaudan.") They are further removed from each other sociologically (and genetically) by the husband's father's illegitimacy—his father is unknown—and by the fact that the husband's mother is a non-Bagnard.

The definition of incest is based on religious prohibitions, but these are interpreted by the people genetically. First-cousin marriage is permitted but not encouraged because of possible deleterious genetic effects in offspring, from the point of view of a Brusonin. In fact, the informal incest prohibition extends, in lessening degree, to all people one calls "cousins"—this group extending, in actual reckoning, to second cousins. Beyond this point, kinship may be acknowledged to exist but it cannot be specified easily or at all, and the marriage prohibition is lifted—especially when the family names of the prospective bride and groom are different. In one such case, for instance, a woman was aware of some kinship ties between her family and that of her fiancé but could not specify them. This awareness, however, taken together with that fact that his brother's behavior was considered abnormal (*malade*) caused her concern about going through with the marriage.

On the social landscape, the familles—especially the six core familles—are often spoken of as being "*nombreuses*." This reveals clearly the distinction between famille and ménage. While it is true that the core familles outnumber the others by two to one, their ménages are, in fact, smaller than those of non-core familles. Although core family names are represented in the same two-to-one proportion in all types of ménages (nuclear and extended families, and remnant nuclear families), they actually make up 75 percent of all ménages with children. The average number of children, however, in a core ménage is lower than that in a non-core ménage (3.3 compared with 4.3). Thus, more core ménages *have* children, but they have fewer each than do non-core ménages.

Historically, as I have already shown, the familles existed at the time of the ancêtres and have come down to the present when they exist in a kind of parallel structure to the set of parentés that make up the village. The familles of today are those whose names have survived. In theory, every family name is potentially that of a famille. Following a two-generation rule of genealogical memory, a name which survives over that period of time is considered the name of a famille, while its individual bearers may be forgotten. Thus, the Morands and Carrons are extinct familles—even though there are living descendants in the village today.

A child born in 1969 is two generations removed from his grandfather born in 1910. One must remember, however, that the census data for 1910 and 1969 encompass more than two generations. The oldest person in the 1969 census is 90 years old, or three to four generations removed from the child born in 1969. The individual born in 1910 still remembers his grandparents born about 1850. This person's *grandparents*, to his grandchildren, are already ancêtres, being five generations removed in time. There is, then, a historical relativism connected with the familles which depends on the age of the person speaking. As long as the family name persists, the famille survives, and, after several generations have passed, it acquires the additional attribute of membership among the ancêtres. Thus, within any famille, one man's *grandparent* may be another's ancêtre—that is, not a particular individual from whom descent can be traced, but the common genealogical property of all Brusonins.

This relativism is the key to a basic distinction between family, or parenté, and famille. Family is an egocentric unit, defined by taking as a reference point one particular individual in his relationships to others; parenté, then, varies with each Ego chosen. Famille, on the other hand, is a socio-centric unit which does not depend on any individual but is rather a structural feature of the society as a whole (Service 1962). As such, it provides cultural continuity—in spite of genealogical amnesia. Because of the temporal overlap between parenté and famille, the two-generation rule of genealogical memory is perfectly adequate: where an individual's genealogical memory ends, the structural principle takes over. Although there are data to indicate that the six core familles and some of the group of fourteen present in both 1910 and 1969 have very long histories in the valley, the cosmological system of familles does not require such historical evidence, and no one claims to know which of the familles were actually the founding ancêtres of Bruson.

Famille, then, is an idealization of parenté, which, in its turn, is an abstraction of ménage. The famille—a socio-centric unit—is essentially a patrinomial descent group whose preservation, manifest in the continuity of its name over time, depends on the reckoning of descent through males. The parenté—an ego-centric unit—is a cognatic descent group composed of members of related familles, or patrilines. The parenté of an unmarried individual is determined by tracing descent through both men and women—specifically, through his mother and his father. An individual brings the parenté to his marriage when it is grafted onto the parenté of his wife. Thus, with the creation of a new ménage, a new parenté comes into existence. Since an individual's parenté includes both lineal and collateral relatives—distinguished by residence either as members of his own ménage (lineals) or as *parents* (collaterals and married siblings who live in different ménages)—the new ménage recognizes this distinction terminologically: the parenté of the new ménage consists of affines (the spouse's lineal relatives) and a combined group of "adopted" *parents*.

The new ménage has special relations with its affines—in the converging family. From the point of view of the two parent ménages, the new ménage is simply their lineal extension with a shift in residence: that is, the new ménage, in addition to encompassing a unique cognatic descent group—a parenté—also takes its place in a patrinomial descent group—a famille. The children of the new ménage will inherit the name of the famille from their father and their kinship network from the combined parenté of both parents. While the parenté is unique to a ménage, its family name is usually shared with others. Since kinship, more or less distant, is imputed to all members of a famille, there is an ideological merging of the familles, at some distant point in the past, into a group of ancestors common to all villagers. By virtue of the ancêtres, the entire village is a common-descent group.

Bruson, then, consists of individuals, each of whom is a member of a ménage and of two converging family units. Each ménage is distinguished by a unique parenté. The village can be said to consist of a set of overlapping parentés corresponding in number to the number of ménages. But there is also a parallel and invisible structure of familles, these being descendants of the common ancestors of the village. It is through these familles that Bruson is distinguished from other villages: just as a parenté is unique to a ménage, so the familles are unique to the village. Brusonins, having these familles in common, form a single kinship unit with respect to the outside world. The familles constitute a kind of meta-parenté, transcending the individual Brusonin and bonding him to his fellow villagers.

11. Family and Responsibility

I have discussed the attribution of neutral or positive qualities to the *familles*. These qualities reverberate down from the cosmological level of *ancêtres* to the contemporary representatives of the familles. As temporal proximity and, therefore, actual acquaintance increases, the attributions become less neutral and more specific personally. As this occurs, however, the emphasis on famille is replaced by an emphasis on the individual member. This is especially true when distinctly negative qualities are attributed to a member of one of the established familles. An individual may be attacked through his family—his *ménage* or his *parenté*—but not so easily through his famille, which is, after all, not his personal domain but the collective tradition of the village.

A further distinction is made in that certain attacks on individuals are considered proper while others are not. Propriety rests on the question of responsibility. A person should not be attacked or ridiculed for something which is not within his control. An individual is not prejudged for or held guilty by association with some negative quality in his family for which he is not responsible. Such an attack is even more reprehensible if it occurs in public—in the café, for instance. Effectively, this means that all attacks on individuals—whether or not through the medium of their families—are personal attacks. Several illustrations will make these distinctions clear.

One evening in the café, a man accused his companion of having insanity in his famiy. The counterattack was, "You make your wife work like a servant." Both statements were based on fact: a relative of this man was institutionalized for mental disease; the wife of the other was known to work very hard, even doing some of the heavy work usually reserved for men, while her husband spent a great deal of time drinking in the café. The initial attack, however, was considered improper, since that fact of mental illness was outside the man's control. On the other hand, the counterattack was perfectly admissible to the argument, since this man's treatment of his wife is his responsibility. Because of this basic imbalance in the argument—and because of the serious implications of introducing family matters—there was bad feeling between the two men for a long time. Finally, after a private apology by the man who had made the improper attack, normal relations were resumed.

By way of contrast, I will cite another argument in the café which—because of the propriety of attacks and the avoidance of introducing family—was more simply resolved. A very drunk client loudly and insistently accused the *patron* of owing him five francs and of being too stingy to pay. The patron denied the charge and managed to ignore the shouting for a few minutes. Finally, seeing that everyone else in the café was aware of it, he smiled knowingly at the others. The smile was a form of diversionary counterattack, expressing, "We all know how mean [*méchant*] Paul is when he's drunk." But the shouting and accusations continued. Since debt, as I have already demonstrated, is intolerable to a Brusonin, the patron felt the need to defend himself and unequivocally to demonstrate his innocence of the charge. He went ostentatiously to the cash register, took out a five-franc coin, and put it on the table in front of his accuser. He then sat down with him, and they drank wine together quietly. In this incident, the attack and counterattack were based on personal qualities for which the individuals could be held responsible. There was, thus, a balanced propriety in the argument, and the final resolution was made in the ménage idiom of drinking together.

In public attacks, the question of responsibility overrides the context of the accusation. In the two accusations made through the vehicle of family, for instance, the one for which the individual cannot be held responsible is considered an improper attack, no matter how true or how damning, and calls for an apology. As illustration of this principle, I cite two items appearing in the gossip-sheet published anonymously in the valley at Mardi Gras time.

1. *Jeunes gens et jeunes filles, pour un mariage catholique et à l'essai, venez passer vos weekends à Bruson, en prenant la 'Liberté'; après une dizaine d'années, vous pourrez recevoir le sacrement sans crainte.*

   (Boys and girls, for a trial marriage that is Catholic, come and spend your weekends in Bruson, taking 'Freedom'; after about ten years, you will be able to receive the sacrament without fear.)

This item refers to the ménage occupying a house named "Liberté." The word "freedom" is used here in two senses: to identify the particular ménage occupying the house of that name, and to attack the parental couple of the ménage through one of its members, a son who has been engaged for several years, and who shows no sign of ever marrying the girl. His behavior reflects on his parents' ménage, and the responsibility for this behavior is therefore extended to his parents who seem to condone it. The attack is not only proper but particularly effective since it evokes a reciprocal responsibility on the part of the individual and of his ménage.

2. *Pour résoudre le problème de la régulation des naissances sans frais et sans désobéir à la dernière encyclique, Jeanette vous propose une excellente formule: pas de pilules contraceptives mais un mari contraceptif.*

   (To solve the problem of birth control without expense and without disobeying the latest Encyclical, Jeanette proposes an excellent formula to you: not contraceptive pills but a contraceptive husband.)

This item refers to a married but childless couple. The wife (Jeanette), although universally liked, is considered deviant in certain ways. She is *indépendante* in ways unbecoming to a woman: she does not go to Mass very often, her dress is a bit too fashionable for a "serious" wife, and she occasionally goes to the café with her husband to play cards. It is generally believed that her husband is to blame for the childlessness—hence the reference to a "contraceptive husband." This gossip item, then, is a double attack on the husband's virility. He is attacked directly for his presumed sterility—an improper attack since he is not responsible—and also, by extension, for his failure as a man to keep his wife in line—this being by itself a perfectly proper accusation.

These two items of gossip were received very differently by Brusonins, including those who were under attack. The first item was found amusing, and even members of the ménage in question weakly laughed about it since they could not deny its propriety or its truth. The second item, however, met with strong general disapproval, and the man in question loudly and publicly denounced the unknown writer of the item. The general feeling was that an injustice had been done: one cannot attack a man for something over which he has no control, and—amplifying the impropriety—one certainly cannot extend this improper accusation to other areas of his life.

Any attack or insult, no matter how outrageous, is permissible as long as it meets the criterion of propriety based on individual responsibility. As an amusing perversion of this principle, there is the case of a woman who, in the course of heated discussion, exasperatedly accused her male companion of being "twisted" in his reasoning—*"tu es une espèce de tordu."* As it happened, this man had a physical handicap which caused him to drag one leg in a twisted fashion behind him. He understood the insult as being directed at his handicap, for which he was not responsible, and, feeling very ill-used, he avoided the woman for several weeks. When a mutual friend explained the situation to her, she immediately went to the man and apologized: "I didn't mean you were twisted physically—just mentally." He accepted the apology, and good relations resumed.

This principle of responsibility as a criterion for the propriety of attacks may be viewed as a product of Catholic teachings. Reprehensible acts of man are explained by his innate moral weakness—*la faiblesse humaine*—and are to be pitied and forgiven. Unfortunate acts of God, however—insanity or infertility—are expressions of His incomprehensible power. God can never, by definition, be guilty, while man is, by his nature, always in a state of guilt. In the same way, religion is pure and perfect, but the church—its temporal and human representative on earth—is fallible and imperfect.

The familles—being responsible for the creation and continuity of the village—are characterized by the same kind of sanctity attributed to God and religion and are equally immune to attack. This fact is dramatized by the open disrespect shown for persons bearing family names which are not well established as familles. In these cases, the family and its individual members are equated, and negative qualities of one are attributed by association to the other. Each individual is held responsible for the failures of all, as well as for the unfortunate events in which human responsibility cannot be assigned. The rules of attack and the criterion of responsibility are suspended with respect to such a family. The characteristics attributed to the family and to its individual members are interchangeable and lead to prejudiced discrimination. The family is not and never will be one of the sacred familles of Bruson.

12. Inheritance

Two systems—the individual kinship network and the village-wide kinship structure—provide the context for inheritance. Through the medium of *parenté*, the individual inherits a unique identity and a supporting property base. From his father he receives *bourgeoisie* in the commune, a family name associated with the village, and a political affiliation associated with that family name. Thus, for example, he is a Bagnard, a Roserens, and a member of the Radical Party. The village as a unit inherits, from the *ancêtres* and the *familles,* a collective identity and an exclusive territory.

The village identity has two parts. First of all, it is a vocation: agriculture. This was the vocation that the ancêtres practiced, the vocation that has made Bruson famous in the patois poetry and proverbs of Bagnes: "It's the land of potatoes! They used to say that you had to pull them up with a crowbar, they were so big." Or, "Bruson—where the beans really grow!" When a villager was asked how he would describe Bruson, he spoke of this peasant vocation and of its underlying ideology:

First of all, its location: on the left bank of the Dranse, on a plateau, a terrace. The fields surround the village, and there are many cultivated fields. It's the most agricultural village in the valley. . . . When you speak of Bruson, you speak especially of

100

the land, and, then too, of the vines in Fully. Most Bruson families have kept their vines, while other villages have mostly abandoned theirs. You can say that Bruson is the village that has remained most attached to the land.

The village identity is also a collective personality. Brusonins are open and friendly people who hospitably open their *ménages* to all. Their sociability is expressed in public by drinking together in the café. They admire eloquence—even if it depends on a certain concentration of alcohol in the bloodstream, as it does for some individuals. They are not *renfermés* (reserved) and silent, like the people of Sarreyer. Following in the tradition of the ancêtres, they grow their own grapes—*le bon Fendant*—and drink most of the harvest themselves. For the men of Bruson, wine-drinking is associated with every activity. As an expression of the ménage principle in the public arena, it is highly ritualized. As an aspect of the collective vocation, it is a frequent topic of conversation: discussion of how the weather this summer will affect the harvest; anecdotes about Bagnards who outwitted the cantonal collectors of the *eau-de-vie* tax.

As an identifying feature of Bruson, wine-drinking is a frequent theme in folktales and humor. A patois poem tells of two friends, returning from a few days' work in their vineyards in Fully, who stopped at a café on the way home to "*boire un verre.*" They had so much to drink that they mistakenly mounted one another's animals for the trip home. The mule and the horse, each carrying the wrong man, arrived safely home, but the men realized their mistake only the next morning, each waking up in the other's house.

Wine-drinking as an essential feature of the collective personality is also expressed in daily speech, as shown in the following examples:

The standard patois greeting as one enters the café:
"*Vo va ti? Tiè tè que tè bai?*"
("How are you? What will you have to drink?")

A statement in patois on the subject of the Brusonin's virility and his esteem in the eyes of his fellows:
"*Selate, po itre considero, fo baire dè vin.*"
("Here, to be respected, you have to drink wine.")

A remark made to me at a public dance (on which occasion even
women are expected to drink) after I had refused wine:
"Soyez de Bruson! Buvez un verre!"
("Be a Brusonin! Have a drink!")

The two aspects of the collective personality of Brusonins—
their hospitable and friendly nature, and their wine tradition—
are beautifully expressed in the following patois statement
which I elicited by asking an informant to teach me something
to say in patois that would please people:

*"Yè mè plise ben selate, i dzin son dè bon diable. Mè fi plèsi,
iè na que prinz'on de bourte cwaïte."*
("I like it here a lot, the people are nice. It pleases me to see
that there are some who get drunk often.")

The importance of wine-drinking—its mythology, its rituals,
and its function as a measure of Brusonin (particularly male)
identity—is based on the peasant vocation which, in turn,
depends on the possession of an exclusive territory. This territory and the collective identity arising from it are Bruson's
legacy from the ancêtres—those legendary common ancestors
who first settled and farmed the land and whose language,
traditions, and identity are embodied today in the familles.
Thus, Bruson is a collectivity not only with respect to its
component ménages—the "one family" concept I discussed
earlier—but also with respect to the larger world. In this
context, the individual Brusonin has no unique identity but
is a representative of the village collectivity. Within the village,
however, his identity depends on his manipulation of the basic
attributes and property which he receives through inheritance
from his parents: his family name, his bourgeoisie, his political
party, and his lands and other possessions.

Inheritance in Bruson is strictly partible, with no preference
either for age or for sex. The *partage*, or apportioning of
property, is made, ideally, before the parents' death, at a period
in their lives when they can no longer work the land. They
divide each kind of property into equal parts, one for each
child—fields, pastures, *mayens*, *vignes*, livestock, and buildings.
The children draw lots to determine their share, and the partage
is then legalized and recorded in the commune. If a child is

not satisfied with the drawing, believing that the shares are not equal, he may ask for a repetition of the process before it has been legalized. Or he may accept the partage but bear hard feelings toward his siblings—often for the rest of his life. No family is immune to the possibility of inheritance *chicanes* (quarrels), and there are a number of people in the village who have not spoken to siblings for twenty years, since the partage was made.

After the partage is made, the parents retain usufructory rights to the property, and, in fact, no child comes into his inheritance fully until both parents are dead. If there are no children, the property passes to close relatives—siblings or siblings' children. It is also possible for an individual to write a will, giving precise instructions for the inheritance of his property after his death. This will, however, may not violate certain legal principles of inheritance—particularly the principle that legitimate children may not be disinherited. An illegitimate child has no claims on the property unless his father has "recognized" him: the father need only acknowledge that this is his child but need not give him his name. A will, then, is often a vehicle for "recognition." An illegitimate child who is not "recognized" inherits only from his mother.

The system of partible inheritance is supported by Swiss law, but the law (in its 1962 revision) sets lower limits on the size of land parcels which may be transferred. These limits are not honored by Brusonins, since they conflict with the ideology of equal inheritance. But this does not mean that property is infinitely divided over time. A control on partibility is the fact that most kinds of property are considered unitary (Weinberg 1972). The units, however, are small and numerous. Land parcels are measured in *mesures*, standardized by the commune at 400 square meters. (In Fully, a different commune where the Brusonin has his vignes, the mesure is about 500 square meters.) A Brusonin speaks of his land holdings in terms of location and surface area in mesures (or, occasionally, half-mesures). That his property may be divided spatially among a number of small parcels scattered over that landscape does not disturb him. In fact, this is often advantageous and recognized as such because of the tremendous ecological variation of the Bruson territory.

Given the limited labor force and the impossibility of large-scale mechanization in this mountain environment, the Brusonin maximizes his agricultural success by controlling a variety of types of land in this miniaturized ecology. For example, he plants strawberries on a total of 4 1/2 mesures divided into three parcels, two in the Condemine region and one in Les Cheneaux. The Condemine being a flat area just below the village, these strawberries mature a week or two earlier than those in the steeper and higher Cheneaux. At the time that he begins harvesting the Cheneaux strawberries, he is also cutting hay in fields nearby. Thus, he distributes his labor and the profits from it over a longer period of time—six weeks instead of four, in the case of strawberries—and he manages to carry out two crop harvests at the same time.

The complete *exploitation*, in the eyes of a Brusonin, consists of some of each of the following kinds of land:

champs	cultivated fields planted to forage crops (potatoes, beets, rutabagas) and market crops (strawberries, raspberries)
prés	hayfields
mayens	intermediate pastures
jardins potagers	kitchen gardens
vignes	vineyards

Many people also own a few fruit trees, but they no longer maintain them and harvest only haphazardly whatever fruit is borne.

In the rare event that parents do not own enough units of land to pass on one of each kind to each child, special arrangements may be made. A child who is intellectually gifted and wishes to enter a profession may receive, as his inheritance, the cost of his higher education. Children interested in agriculture will receive livestock and at least a minimal share in the land required to support the animals, as well as the structures for housing them (barns) and for storing their hay and forage (*granges*, or in patois, *raccards*). The children who receive livestock inherit, along with the animals, membership in one of the *consortages* whose *alpage* lands, though owned by the *bourgeois* of Bagnes, are traditionally associated with Bruson. In this instance, then, individual and village inheritance converge—the village inheriting lands from the ancêtres, and the individual inheriting usufructory rights in those lands through his parenté.

In any case, the shares of all the children are calculated to be equivalent in monetary terms and are sometimes actually converted into money. These adjustments are made, sometimes long after the partage, among the children themselves as each pursues his individual career and decides what part of the inheritance is most valuable to him. In one such case, a man exchanged with his brother a mayen for some vignes, making up the monetary difference in cash. This man operates a café and keeps only a few cows. His brother, an engineer in Lausanne, wanted land on which to build a vacation house and was perhaps also looking ahead to an eventual sale of this property to tourists.

The inheritance of dwellings presents problems, since it is acknowledged that a house cannot usefully be split into an indefinite number of parts. Also relevant to this question is the requirement that each ménage have its own kitchen. In the best situation, there are two or three separate and complete apartments in the house, but, even in this case, there may be more than two or three potential heirs. The parents' decision as to how to divide the house is again based on the particular needs of each child, as seen by the parents. A married daughter living in her husband's house may be disqualified, while a child who is not married and is past marriageable age is a likely heir of at least part of the house. If, however, there is any doubt as to the needs of the children—either with respect to land or buildings—the partage is made on a strictly equal basis and adjustments come later as they become necessary.

This is, in fact, the most frequent occurrence—the equal partage—and explains why chicanes are expected as a matter of course. Adjustment among the heirs themselves, an alternative to chicane, takes the form either of exchanging or of "buying back" (*racheter*) pieces of property. That this "buying back" is thought of as a familistic exchange rather than a commercial transaction is evidenced by the phrase *racheter avec*—buying back *with*, not *from*: "*il a racheté la maison avec ses frères*" (meaning "he bought out his brothers' shares in the house").

These exchanges of property among heirs also reflect a recognition of the essential unity of ménage property. Along with the ideology of equal shares—a dispersing force—there is a feeling for the integrity of an exploitation which acts as another control on infinite partibility. This feeling is consistent with successful farming in a marginal environment. It is clearly understood that, not only must an individual have a variety of types of land, but he must also have enough of each type. If his share of the inheritance is quantitatively or qualitatively lacking, measured against his view of a workable exploitation, he will have to supplement it in some way. His best course of action is to effect an exchange with a sibling who is not interested in agriculture or who is already farming land that his wife has inherited. Such an exchange—as, for instance, the case cited earlier of a mayen for a vineyard—eliminates the need for a large cash investment. But even when cash is involved—when a man buys out his siblings' shares in land, for example—he is acquiring land that he knows intimately and, thus, can cultivate most effectively.

Exchanges or cash transactions of this sort—within the group of heirs—occur in every generation. While equal division of the property is an essential principle of inheritance, maintenance of an effective exploitation is essential to successful agriculture. Exchanges of inheritance shares effect this consolidation of property and counteract the dispersing force of strict partibility.

The exploitation that is inherited and then perfected through manipulation—first by the inclusion of other family lands and the absorption of the wife's inheritance, and later perhaps by the purchase of lands outside the parenté—eventually comes up, in its turn, for partage. The individual himself—in his lifetime a member of a parenté—eventually becomes an ancêtre, a nameless member of one of the familles, and his ménage property continues to exist as a part of the exclusive territory of Bruson.

13. A Case Study in Inheritance

I have outlined inheritance patterns both for the individual Brusonin and for the village collectivity. I have shown that these systems, running parallel and sometimes converging, generate individual and village identities, both supported by a land and property base. In order to illuminate this dual structure, I shall now consider a particular case of inheritance for which the data are extensive, both in time and in space.

In 1910 a village census was made by a Brusonin who is the paternal grandfather of a member of the present population. Damien Deslarzes was then sixty-seven. He had grown up in a house built in 1835 by his father Eugène and his mother Catherine Maret. This house still stands and bears the builders' initials and the year of construction engraved in the stone over the entrance. About 1850, François Morand built a house attached to Eugène's.

The history of these houses and their occupants is based, in part, on genealogical and census data. Where such data were not available, I have supplied a reconstruction, based on information received from descendants of these families who now

107

occupy the house and from others in the village. This reconstruction rests on two incontrovertible but apparently contradictory facts: first, the structure built by Eugène Deslarzes
and François Morand, acting independently and at different
times, is now known universally as "the house of Floride
Deslarzes"; second, six of its present seven inhabitants bear
the name Maret, and the seventh, a Deslarzes, is not an owner
or heir of the property.

Eugène Deslarzes was born around 1800, one of eight children. Eugène's brother Benjamin emigrated to America in 1849,
farming in Wisconsin and raising six children by two wives.
He tried to persuade Eugène to join him, writing letters at
long intervals over a period of forty-seven years. Eugène's
great-grandson, living in Bruson today, has preserved these
letters and has painstakingly copied them into a notebook. The
set includes a letter written by a son of Benjamin who com-
plains to his aunt in Le Sappey that his father cheated him
out of his inheritance, giving it all to the children of his second
marriage. In 1892, when Benjamin received the news of his
sister's death in Le Sappey, he wrote to a nephew in Bagnes
inquiring about "his share" in the inheritance:

> . . . one field and two pastures, as well as some furniture, all
> worth 1431 francs. I hurriedly replied [to the notary] to tell him
> that he could send me the money as soon as it was available.
> I have received nothing since, neither money nor news. I dare
> to hope that you will not let me wait too long for news and
> that you can perhaps tell me if this money should be coming
> to me one day and approximately when.

The great-grandson especially prizes these letters, saying in
amusement that, even then, inheritance was the major source
of *chicanes* within a family.

Eugène Deslarzes was the only one of the siblings to remain
in Bruson. By 1910, of course, Eugène and his wife were long
dead, but there were in the village seventeen direct lineal
descendants bearing the Deslarzes name and six direct descendants through Deslarzes women. These twenty-three individuals, living in six different *ménages*, made up 5 percent of
the total population (423) and 5 percent of the total number
of ménages in the village (109)—an indication that the Deslarzes

ménages were about average in size compared with other ménages of the time.

Among these Deslarzes was Eugène's son Damien, our census-taker. His daughter would later marry her first cousin, Damien's sister's son. First-cousin marriage required, as it still does, the purchase of a special dispensation from the church. Brusonins of today, at least, are wary of such a marriage for genetic reasons—which they do not fully understand but which they believe are unfortunately manifest in the children of certain closely-related couples they know. Whenever the Deslarzes first-cousin marriage is spoken of, there is evident relief in the accompanying statement that this marriage was childless.

Damien's brother Valentin, dead by 1910, had inherited his father's house which was now occupied by two of Valentin's children, adult but unmarried. One of these was Floride Deslarzes, after whom the house is now named. Damien's sister had four children, one of whom married into a nearby village. Her son—the great-grandson of Eugène Deslarzes—returned to Bruson twenty-three years later to marry a Bruson woman. It is he, Jean Fellay, who preserved the letters from America of Eugène's brother Benjamin. Although Jean grew up in another village, he knows Bruson very well because "we used to come and help our grandparents"—an instance of a converging family work-group extending even beyond village limits.

Compared with the Deslarzes of 1910, the direct lineal descendants of François Morand were few. Of his seven children, only four had remained in Bruson. One of them, already married in 1910, stayed in the village but had no descendants beyond his own children. Two other daughters, no longer living in Bruson in 1910, had left behind two illegitimate children. One of these Morand daughters, after having her illegitimate child, had married a man from a nearby commune and raised eight children there. By marrying out of the commune, she had lost her *bourgeoisie*. Her legitimate children, then, were not Bagnards, and, even though they were direct lineal descendants of a Brusonin, Damien never added them to his census. Her illegitimate daughter, whose father is believed to have been a transient Italian worker, was later to marry Damien's grandson.

Thus, the François Morand ménage in 1910 consisted of three adult unmarried daughters and two illegitimate grandchildren. One of the daughters was soon to marry Floride Deslarzes, who lived in the other half of the attached house. Their daughter would eventually marry a villager and inherit her mother's part of the house built by François Morand. These, then, were the descendants of François Morand living in Bruson in 1910: ten individuals living in two ménages—one of which was the original parental ménage and the other created by a marriage.

François' illegitimate granddaughter, who married Damien Deslarzes' grandson, inherited her mother's share in the house and, eventually, the shares of her mother's sisters after their deaths. One of these aunts lived in the city for a few years and returned to Bruson in 1920 to establish the café which today takes up about half the ground-floor level of François Morand's house.

The café, the small general store that used to exist in the adjoining room, and the second-floor apartment are today the inheritance of Rosy Maret, the daughter of François Morand's illegitimate granddaughter. The third-floor apartment is the inheritance of Josephine Maret, François Morand's granddaughter. These two women—the only remaining descendants of François Morand today (with the exception of Josephine's children)—are first cousins once-removed, but their husbands, both Marets, are not known to be related.

Yet a third Maret—Céline Maret née Baillifard—owns an apartment in the house built by Eugène Deslarzes. Céline, at ninety the oldest Brusonin, is widowed and lives most of the year with a married daughter in another village. For this reason—her inaccessibility—and because of her age, it was difficult to trace her genealogy and thereby explain her inheritance of the apartment. The most likely reconstruction I could make was that she is the granddaughter of Eugène Deslarzes' wife's sister, and, thus, a second cousin of Floride Deslarzes. Since Eugène probably built the house upon his marriage, it was considered the joint property of the couple, and, thus, part of it could have passed to his wife's sister and her heirs.

In any case, these three Maret women, two of them descendants of François Morand and the third perhaps descended from

Eugène Deslarzes' wife's sister, are today the owners of what is called "the house of Floride Deslarzes." One woman is actually Floride's daughter, and the other is his wife's sister's granddaughter. The only Deslarzes living in the house, although he is Floride's first cousin's son, is not in the line of inheritance for the house and lives there only by virtue of his marriage to a Morand. In addition, the only part of this structure that was ever the property of Floride Deslarzes is now unoccupied.

This case study of "the house of Floride Deslarzes" and of the two families which have occupied it is only a particular example illustrating certain standard situations in Bruson, prevalent both today and in the past. Basic to these is the genesis and survival of a *famille*, and, as a corollary, the Brusonin's intense interest in kinship. Damien Deslarzes' 1910 census is one example of this interest but not, by any means, a unique example. In 1962, Damien's grandson Pierre— an only child—made a similar census of the village. When Pierre observed my interest in genealogy—admittedly based on a different set of motivations—he begged me to trace his personal family tree as far back in time as possible. He had himself attempted to do this, using his grandfather's 1910 census and other documents, but—due to lack of time, information, and method—he had never succeeded. He gave me what documents he had and put me in touch with people who could supplement this information—members of non-Bagnes branches of the family, a relative who is the Town Clerk of the commune and has access to the census registry, and his two aunts who are in their seventies and the informal genealogical experts of the village.

The aunts—or, *"les Tantes,"* as they are called universally— are, in fact, the aunts or great-aunts of a majority of living Brusonins. Because of age and infirmity (one is almost totally blind and the other almost totally deaf), they rarely leave their house but often receive visitors—their many nephews and nieces who feel bound to call on them occasionally. Many of these even address the aunts in the polite form (*vous*)—something unheard of within the kinship structure of the entire village— out of respect for their age. One of the aunts never married and lived in Marseilles for forty years, working in hotels and

ultimately returning to her natal village. The other is the
woman mentioned earlier who married her first cousin and was
childless. But, though unmarried and childless, the aunts do
not lack for kinship relations. They are, in fact, a kind of anchor
and reference point in the village-wide kinship structure—both
because of their actual kin, children and grandchildren of
siblings, and because of their membership in the Deslarzes
famille.

The family tree I finally produced for Pierre—with the incal-
culable aid of a computer—is the most sophisticated such
document to exist in Bruson (D. and G. M. Weinberg 1972).
Others have been made by Brusonins, handwritten in note-
books. One such genealogy goes back about 150 years and
includes such items of supplementary information as:

Jean (illégitime reconnu)—a "recognized" illegitimate son
Maurice, pas marié (sourd)—not married, deaf
William, marié Michellod de Villette, à Paris—married a Michel-
   lod of Villette, in Paris
*Jean-Marie et Louis, morts célibataires à la fleur de leur
   vie*—died unmarried in the prime of life
*Maurice, Eugène et une fille—les trois bonaces, pas marié*s
   (illetrés)—all three feeble-minded, unmarried, illiterate
Benjamin, mort célibataire (mal caduc)—died unmarried, epilep-
   tic
Casimir, célibataire (nain)—unmarried, dwarf
Ernest, mort accidentellement dans les rochers, près Fionnay—
   died accidentally on the rocks near Fionnay
Marcel, marchand de bétail—cattle merchant
*Delphine, fille-mère. Delphine a marié très tard Joseph Frioud,
   Fribourgeois (soulon), pas d'enfants*—unwed mother.
   Delphine, very late, married Joseph Frioud of Fribourg,
   a drunkard, no children

These people are, for better or for worse, one's ancestors;
they make up the famille in question and, as such, take their
place in the kinship structure of the entire village. In this
particular case, their individual names, achievements, and
destinies are recorded. In the typical case, however, where no
such record exists (except, of course, scattered throughout the
commune registry), the genealogical memory of contemporary
Brusonins is only about two generations deep. Beyond that

time span, an individual is either forgotten or merged with the ancêtres. His fate, in the village memory, depends on whether or not he is a member of a famille—that is, of a surviving parenté whose name continues to exist through time. This is clearly demonstrated in the Deslarzes-Morand history. The house takes its present name from an individual who lived there two generations ago and whose family name has survived. There are no Morands in the village today, and, in fact, only one of the Deslarzes—an old man—lives in "the house of Floride Deslarzes." One may speculate with some justification that, sixty years from now, it will be called "the Maret house."

This recognition of the relative permanence of certain family names and the obliteration of others—based on factors of time and famille status—is shown in the naming of other village houses. One house, for instance, was built in 1782 by a man named Carron—a member of an illustrious and then widespread family whose descendants included commune officials and physicians. It is occupied today by a childless couple, the husband a non-bourgeois named Allaman and the wife—the owner of the house—whose maiden name is not Carron but Rappaz. In referring to the house, Brusonins exhibit some confusion: "It's the Carron house—that is, the house of Marie Rappaz." Marie Rappaz's mother was a Carron—a direct descendant of the builder of the house—but the name no longer exists in Bruson. The name of the house is, at this moment in time, in a transitional state. Following the two-generation rule of genealogical memory, it is properly called "the Carron house." But the famille Carron, having no living representatives in Bruson today, is losing its place as a famille. Only because of its past history—in the not-too-distant past—does it still supply the name of this house. One can safely predict that, in the future— perhaps even in the next generation—the Carron origins of the house will be forgotten and it will be called "the house of Marie Rappaz."

House-building is still practiced in Bruson today, although modern Brusonins tend to build on the outskirts of the village, creating new residential *quartiers*, because of the lack of space within the village itself. Most Brusonins, too, express a preference for living in the more open and less steep areas just outside the village—land which was once entirely cultivated. Perhaps this desire for more sunshine in houses and the aesthetic wish to remove them spatially from the manure piles were present in the past as well. The present expression of these ideals, however, is probably new and reflects the modern Brusonin's stated desire to improve certain aspects of his life. Six new houses have been built in the past ten years, but many more have been "redone"—by the installation of running water and interior plumbing, of central heating systems, and of such modern kitchen equipment as washing machines.

The six newly-built houses are—functionally, if not architecturally—very much in the tradition of the past: they were built by married couples—both spouses Brusonins—with children, and they are large enough to accommodate more than a single ménage. In addition, all six ménages are active and successful in agriculture, though three of the husbands have another *métier* as well—schoolteacher, ski instructor, and agricultural extension agent. Three of the ménages are among the largest in Bruson, with six or seven children each, and a fourth, with two children, is probably not yet complete. The family names of all six ménages are among the familles of Bruson, by virtue of their long history and large representation. In sum, then, these six ménages—the house-builders of today—represent Brusonin tradition and express faith in its future.

House-building provides the only means of creating new, substantial, and lasting property—in fact, a heritage for future generations. This underlying motive is also expressed in examples of "redoing" existing houses in the village by enlarging them or creating new apartments on abandoned floors. Closely related to this desire for adding to the heritage of descendants is a wish to escape the restrictions of one's own inheritance. One couple, for instance, was living with their two young sons in a house still belonging to the wife's father. The husband had inherited no dwelling of his own, and it seemed unlikely that the wife's father would be ready to make a partage of his property for some time to come. Consequently, the couple built a new house, just outside the village, large enough to accommodate two or, perhaps, three separate ménages. It was clearly their intention to provide housing for their sons when they married. Just before the new house was completed, the older son was killed in a motorcycle accident, and the general reaction was—what a shame to have built such a large house when there was now only one possible heir.

House-building represents a high-risk venture into immortality. Sons may die, or never marry, or marry out of the village—as I have shown in the Deslarzes-Morand history. As in the Morand situation, most of the heirs may be daughters through whom the family name is lost. Whatever the sex of the heirs, there is no guarantee that they will remain in the village—whether or not they marry—since the postmarital residence rule has always been based on expedience in each particular case. Expedience, of course, includes inheritance factors, and couples tend to make their residence where they have housing and land. But, since the property holdings of a ménage have never been large enough to support all the heirs, especially if they all married, decisions have had to be made and some heirs have effectively been driven out of the village, their inheritance "bought back" by siblings who remained. Thus, one of the Tantes spent most of her productive life in Marseilles; two of the sons of Eugène Deslarzes married out of the village, as did a grandson and a granddaughter.

Because of the uncertainties of inheritance—one's own decisions about a life career being interdependent with those of one's siblings—there have been many late marriages, a number of couples far apart in age, and a certain proportion of siblings never marrying but living out their lives in the parental ménage. Floride Deslarzes and his wife were, respectively, thirty-eight and thirty-six when they married; François Morand's daughter was twelve years older than her husband; Damien Deslarzes' ménage in 1910 included four unmarried children between the ages of twenty-four and thirty-five—only one of whom was ever to marry; Valentin Deslarzes' ménage was in 1910 what one may call a "remnant nuclear family" consisting of three unmarried children in their thirties, both parents now dead. In Bruson, the terms "*vieux garçon*" (bachelor) and "*vieille fille*" (spinster) are household words. However, although there are sixty-four unmarried adult individuals in the village (forty-five men and nineteen women), all those up to about the age of forty are considered still marriageable and the terms are not applied to them. In fact, only twenty of these sixty-four individuals (thirteen men and seven women) are over forty—an

indication that emigration has been a frequent alternative to
marriage. In a recent and extreme example in violation of this
principle, a man of forty-nine, by then considered a *vieux
garçon*, married a non-Brusonin woman of twenty-four.

A by-product of late marriage is the high frequency of
children conceived—and sometimes born—out of wedlock. Of
the forty-one married women living in Bruson today for whom
there are reliable data, ten—about 25 percent—bore their first
child less than seven months after the marriage. Great value
is placed on marriage in such cases, and, if the father resists
or denies fatherhood, suit is brought against him. If the suit
is successful, he is required to marry the girl or pay an indem-
nity. At the time of the suit, the girl must reveal the names
of all her lovers—that is, of all possible fathers of the child
she is carrying. If there is only one, or if the case is strongest
against one of several, he is held liable. If he chooses not to
marry the girl, the child bears the mother's family name and
is, by custom, raised in the ménage of the mother's parents.
In addition to the example in the Morand family, there are
such cases in the village today.

No stigma is attached to an illegitimate child—François
Morand's illegitimate granddaughter, for instance, married and
remained in Bruson—but the mother's reputation is tarnished,
and she might never marry. If she does, it is likely to be a
marriage outside the village and even outside the commune—as
was the case for François Morand's daughter. As the child grows
up in his grandparents' ménage, he may, with time, come to
be identified with them rather than with his mother. One
Brusonin who is seventy-six years old today—married and with
grandchildren—is known by a patronymic, "Cyrille d'Antoine,"
which refers to his mother's father in whose ménage he was
raised. As another example of the two-generation rule of genealogical memory, many Brusonins today are confused about this
man's parentage, and the younger ones believe that his father's
name was Antoine.

In this detailed examination of a particular inheritance
history—that of "the house of Floride Deslarzes"—I have fo-
cused both on property inheritance and on its wide variety
of implications in the kinship sphere. The Brusonin's intense
interest in his genealogy is but a superficial expression of his

deep awareness of the meaning of kinship. Through the descent line of the famille, he inherits not only a house and other real property but also a name—a family name and perhaps the informal name of the house. The continuity of the famille is expressed concretely in the house and is thereby passed on to future generations. The Brusonin reaffirms his famille status, if necessary, by establishing a new house and property base to be passed down to his descendants. Although this venture involves greater risks today than in the past—because of the changed emphasis on agriculture and the diminished population—these risks are different only quantitatively. Striking the balance between an ideology of strictly partible inheritance and a conception of the integrity of an exploitation remains a major concern and motivation of the Brusonin.

14. Friendship

Considering the Brusonin's initial denial of "best friend" relationships and his eventual characterization of them as existing outside the social system of the village, there is a surprisingly large body of terminology associated with friendship. Not only does friendship exist in Bruson, but it exists in a number of different forms. I have already discussed instrumental and emotional friendship and distinguished these in several ways: their sphere of operation (within or outside the kinship network that embraces the entire village), their affective base (friendliness as opposed to confidence), their relative cost to the individual in personal freedom, and their relationship to marriage and the life cycle.

The terminology of friendship is expressive of some of these categories as well as of certain others which are more basic—sex, age, and marital status. The essential terms of friendship are:

copain (copine)	
	pal, comrade
camarade	
meilleur(e) ami(e)	best friend
grand(e) ami(e)	good friend
bon(ne) ami(e)	boyfriend (girlfriend)

The first two terms imply friendliness and, therefore, fall in the category of instrumental friendship. A copain (to use one of the interchangeable terms in this group) may be a villager or someone outside the village sphere, a relative or a non-kinsman. Copains may be of the same sex or of the opposite sex, and they may constitute a group larger than two. They are usually young unmarried adults who often do things together, although they are not necessarily inextricably associated with one another. A child of school age is theoretically copain with all his fellows. A teenager, out of school, usually has one group of copains. As he grows older and his social contacts broaden—through work or travel—he may be involved in several distinct groups of copains, each one constituting a kind of special-purpose friendship group. He may, for instance, have a copine from another village with whom he skis every week or two; a village copain who owns a motorcycle with whom he makes regular Sunday excursions into the Rhône valley; a group of copains with whom he often plays cards in the café.

The school child and teenager usually form such relationships with persons of their own age group or of their specific *classe*. With increasing age and social contacts, the group of copains may be of different ages, within certain broad limits: that is, a thirty-year-old man will not ordinarily consider a sixty-year-old as his copain. Since the basic criterion is that they be young and unmarried, with the implication that they are still marriageable—that is, under about forty years of age—the age range of a group of copains may be as large as twenty years. This is usually somewhat narrower, however, since those in their early twenties are often still involved in their teenage friendship groups which tend to be more exclusive. Marriage, both for men and for women, puts an end to copain groups—although certain two-person relationships within them may continue to exist in somewhat modified form—and married people speak of others in terms of "he used to be my copain."

Since the copain relationship is a casual one, it gives way easily in the face of the greater demands of marriage and *ménage*. Because copains are defined as people who do things together, their function is supposedly superseded when one enters the more serious and time-consuming state of marriage. Copains are the somewhat frivolous and nonessential compan-

ions of premarital youth. The *meilleur ami* relationship, however, is based on confidence and is recognized as being more
serious and deeply rooted. After marriage, therefore, although
one has less time for a meilleur ami, the affective base of this
emotional friendship—as well as the fact that it always involves
a person of the same sex—presents no threat to the marital
relationship and, in fact, is motivated by a similar seriousness
of attachment.

While the ménage is a closed group with respect to confidence—a private group—it is acknowledged that men and
women have different and sometimes incompatible emotional
needs and interests. Their needs for a same-sex confidante are
respected, as long as this relationship does not interfere with
their marital and ménage duties. In actual practice, however,
many people lose their childhood meilleurs amis to circumstances: the best friend may marry out of the village, for
instance, to return on visits only infrequently if at all. But
while the meilleur ami relationship may become completely
and permanently inactive, the meilleur ami remains a real
person in one's life. One woman, when asked to name her
meilleure amie, named three women: the first was a cousin
living in Le Sappey who had died when both were about
thirteen—"we were inseparable"; the second, a meilleure amie
of young unmarried days, had married and moved to Martigny
and now visits Bruson several times a year; the third, an
acquaintance of only the past five years, is a Frenchwoman
who spent a few months in Bruson doing demographic research
and who returns to ski almost every winter. The meilleur ami
relationship, although inactivated by marriage or circumstances, is never extinguished.

Marriage, however, is not a totally isolating mechanism.
Though it takes its toll of copains and meilleurs amis, it offers
the individual a larger network of instrumental friendships—the
expanded kinship network—and it also offers certain new
friendship possibilities outside of kinship. The *grand ami* is,
in a sense, a postmarital reconstruction of both copains and
meilleurs amis. Grands amis are often friends of the married
couple—usually another married couple. The affective base of
such a relationship may be friendliness or confidence. The
distinguishing feature recalls the definition of copain: grands

amis are people who often do things together. These activities
are, of course, conducted within the context of the two ménages.
Thus, for instance, one couple regularly visits the other to spend
an evening chatting and playing cards. The same two couples
plan and make an annual motoring excursion of two or three
days to some not-too-distant place of interest—the Burgundy
region of France, the Grisons in eastern Switzerland, the Furka
Pass area, or Milan.

It is even possible for an unmarried meilleur ami or copain
of premarital days to become a grand ami of the new ménage.
Most often, this grand ami is a man, continuing his earlier
relationship with the husband. This is simply a manifestation
of the greater freedom of mobility of men in the culture,
whether married or not. A married man is still expected to
appear in the social milieu of the café, though perhaps less
frequently and devotedly than before his marriage. He also
has many opportunities to make extra-village contacts through
his work. His wife, on the other hand, is expected to tend to
her ménage and stay within its physical bounds—especially
when there are children—except for the rare occasions when
she is supposed to be "invited out" by her husband—some
Sundays and holidays and occasional weekend evenings in the
café. She conducts her friendship activities in her kitchen,
during the afternoon when her husband is away at work. Her
husband's old friend—copain or meilleur ami—often visits the
house when the husband is present and also continues the
two-person relationship outside the ménage itself.

The *bon ami* relationship, by definition between two persons
of opposite sex, is very impermanent. It may last a few weeks
or a few years, but it is always terminated—either by simple
dissolution or by marriage of the couple. It is also the least
visible of friendships. Although the couple may, at a certain
point, decide to marry, there is no formal engagement, and
their intention is made known publicly only upon posting of
the banns. They are seen together but most often in larger
groups and, in fact, behave publicly like copains. If a girl's
bon ami is from outside the village, the relationship is more
likely to be known, even though the couple may never actually
be seen together in Bruson. Within the village, however, such
a relationship is easily masked within the group of copains.

Only members of this group are likely to know of the special relationship that exists within it. Once the banns are posted, the villagers realize that this couple has been seen together for some time, though always within the context of a group. If this is not the case, then there is a general assumption that the relationship has been only a private one—that is, sexual—and that the couple is *obligé* to marry by reason of pregnancy. The bon ami relationship, then, is unique among friendships in that it is usually recognized by the community only after the fact.

Associated with this friendship terminology is a set of verbs expressing affect. *Aimer*, as in standard French usage, is restricted in meaning to "love" and in usage to lineal relatives and to the bon ami or spouse. In actual practice, the word is rarely heard—at least not in public. Less committing verbs of affect are *aimer bein* (to like a lot) and *plaire* (to please). One can say of a friend (of any degree), as well as of a favorite food or sport—"*je l'aime bien*" or "*il me plaît.*" "*Estimer*" means "to respect" and can refer to equals or to superiors. It expresses an affect based on intellectual judgment, and the verb is also used to express an opinion on some impersonal and abstract question: "*J'estime mon copain.*" ("I respect my pal.") or "*J'estime que l'agriculture n'a pas d'avenir.*" ("I believe that agriculture has no future.")

There are no explicit terms for negative affect; such feelings or relationships are simply not discussed. The only linguistic evidence of their existence is found in the set of adjectives used to describe people. *Gentil* and *sympathique* are positive qualities of a general descriptive nature. While both words mean "nice," gentil is more neutral and noncommittal and usually refers to a person one knows less intimately. Both words emphasize the described person's membership in the common mainstream of humanity—reassuring one that, at his hands, one will receive the good treatment due any human being. The same connotation is attached to the patois phrase *bon diable* (good devil, or good fellow), implying—he shares my weaknesses and my strengths, and, because of this common ground, he will treat me well.

In another pair of descriptive terms, difference is emphasized. *Unique* and *spécial* both mean "eccentric." *Unique*, however, is a complimentary term while spécial has a derogatory connotation. The eccentricity of *unique* has social value—such a person, for instance, may be known for his wit and is, therefore, entertaining. Spécial, however, implies antisocial eccentricity—strangeness. Its derogatory connotation is usually softened by an understating modifier: in most frequent usage, the term appears as *un peu spécial* (a little strange). When the tolerable limits of antisocial eccentricity are exceeded, the individual has fallen into insanity and is described as *malade* (ill) or suffering a *dépression nerveuse* (nervous depression). Insanity, the extreme case of being spécial, may be a cause or an effect of antisocial behavior. Instances of such behavior which Brusonins offer as examples or effects of insanity include suicide, divorce, promiscuity, kleptomania, and incest.

One current situation which is still on the borderline between eccentric and insane behavior will make this clear. A young man, upon completion of his secondary education in the valley, went to another canton, where he learned three languages and worked as a secretary. He was, thus, obviously *intélligent* and *instruit* (educated)—both admirable qualities. After about four years, he inexplicably returned to Bruson, had nothing to do with his parents or brothers, and took up residence with a non-kin spinster in her eighties. Though he was seen occasionally in public—on trips to the store, for instance—he never spoke to anyone and never entered the café. Eventually, he bought a cow and joined the village *laiterie*. As far as anyone knows, he spends all his time and energy working the old woman's lands. He is regarded as spécial because he has abandoned a good and prestigious job which employed his talents and education for the relatively menial and unremunerative work of agriculture. The condemnation of antisocial behavior rests on his denial of kinship and friendship, motivated, in the villagers' opinion, by a desire for personal and exclusive monetary gain. This behavior cannot be explained within the normal limits of eccentricity, and many villagers wonder if he is not actually malade.

Another pair of descriptive terms refers to specific areas of personality: *intélligent* to the intellect, and *sérieux* to the moral sense. When the terms are used negatively, they express condemnation, again in terms of antisocial behavior. Sérieux is

difficult to translate: it refers to a person's attitude toward
duty. If the context is marriage, then sérieux might mean
hard-working and faithful. A married woman who has lovers
is not *sérieuse*, and is, by implication, contemptible. Even if
unmarried, a woman who is promiscuous in her sexual relationships is not sérieuse, and, by implication, not marriageable.
In the Catholic ethic, however, although one is not required
to marry such a woman, one is impelled to pity her. Thus,
the description is usually associated with an explanation, such
as her lack of intélligence. This, of course, makes an even
stronger case for not marrying the woman.

The quality of intélligence often enters into the description
of a person who is somewhat spécial. Intélligence is the burden
of a few individuals who are expected to behave in an exemplary
manner because of it. This was demonstrated in the example
of the young man who gave up his city job. In another case,
a man who drinks heavily is criticized more harshly than he
would be otherwise, because he is intélligent. Although intélligence is an admirable quality, the word is most often used
in a critical or derogatory sense. In fact, one never speaks of
the lack of intélligence which is perfectly evident in certain
individuals of below-average mental capacity. As long as they
fulfill their duties to ménage and village, they are loved and
indulged.

The vocabulary of friendship and of its counterpart, criticism,
is extensive and precise. Friendship behavior, however, is diffuse, shifting, and not clearly specified. The broad distinction
between instrumental and emotional friendship refers generally
to ties within and ouside of the kinship network. Both kinds
of affective association are necessary to an individual, but,
because of their different spheres of operation, they are usually
kept apart. Because instrumental friendship is associated with
kinship, it is practiced openly. Emotional friendship, however,
is the property of the individual and, thus, a private matter.
This is expressed by the denial of its existence, especially in
its most intense forms of meilleur ami and bon ami.

In apparent violation of these principles of and implicit rules
for conducting friendships, one Brusonin, on the occasion of
his seventy-fifth birthday, invited a small group of friends to
a fondue supper to be held in the small room attached to the

café. I was one of those invited and so observed the event at first hand. The party happened to fall on Mardi Gras which is celebrated with much gaiety, dancing, drinking, and masquerading. Members of the birthday party group arrived at the café and drank apéritifs there, among the Mardi Gras celebrants, while their table was being prepared in the next room—a public room usually reserved for such group meals. Albert, the host, was actually born in another village but came to Bruson at a very early age and has lived there all his life. He married a Brusonin, and they had a son who died young. Albert's wife died in an accident about seven years ago, and he has no relatives in the village.

All his six guests, then, were his friends. Their ages ranged from thirty-three to sixty-three. There were two married couples, one old bachelor, and I. Albert and two of the men in the group were grands amis and probably also, in two-person combinations, meilleurs amis. Albert, of course, was the oldest, and the two men were in the same classe. Albert and Adrien—the bachelor in the group—were *quartier* neighbors. Albert and Louis were fellow members of Alpenrose, the village singing society, and were also very active in the Bruson section of the Conservative Party. Adrien, an age-mate of Louis, was a grand ami of Louis and his wife Jeanne.

The other married couple present, Ernest and Edwina, were quartier neighbors and grands amis of Albert and Adrien. This neighbor relationship also had certain qualities of instrumental friendship in that it was a mutual-aid relationship. My presence was explained by virtue of my activity as accompanist at Alpenrose rehearsals. Because of the disparity of ages and my position as an outsider, it would be difficult to specify what kind of friendship existed between Albert and me. He had great respect for my musical ability, found me sympathique, appreciated my interest in the life of Bruson, and probably would have used the word estimer to describe what he felt for me.

I was well acquainted with Louis and Jeanne, less so with Adrien, and not at all with Ernest and Edwina. The two married couples seemed to have no particular friendship ties except those that existed through the two men who lived alone. Except for the fact that Louis and Adrien were distant cousins, no kinship ties linked members of these five ménages. The three

men in the group who were grands amis were never seen
together in public, in the café for instance, except in connection
with other activities such as Alpenrose functions. Albert would
come into the café almost every evening after supper for his
usual mint tea followed by tea laced with red wine.

Although he was liked and respected, his non-Brusonin
origins were never forgotten. With no kinsmen in the village,
he had no instrumental friendship network and was limited
to emotional friendships of varying origin and degree of intensity. He placed high value on these friendships and was the
only Brusonin I ever heard to speak openly of them. At the
end of the birthday supper, he made a little speech thanking
us all for having come and, thus, expressing our friendship for
him. We had coffee and liqueur after supper in the café, still
crowded with Mardi Gras revelers. Then we continued the party
at Louis' house and finally, in the early hours of morning,
returned to our respective dwellings.

On the next day, two incidents occurred which succinctly
express the paradoxical nature of the birthday party. The first
was a series of greetings exchanged among participants when
they encoutered each other on the street: "Did you sleep well?"
This is a standard greeting which follows an occasion of friendship behavior. The behavior may have been quite public—a card
game in the café, for instance—but it is transformed, with this
greeting, into a private event, indicating the existence of emotional friendship. The greeting itself is neutral and seems to
carry no information beyond what is overtly expressed. Its
covert meaning, however, is clearly understood by the two
individuals as referring to their essentially private interaction
of the evening before. In the context of the birthday party,
then, the underlying and private emotional friendship of the
event was reaffirmed by its participants.

The second incident following the birthday party took place
that afternoon in the same café. Albert was having tea, and
the café owner—a man of sixty-three—joined him in some
embarrassment and expressed his hurt at not having been
invited to the party: "We used to play together as children."
The implication was that Albert, in inviting his friends, had
neglected his childhood copain. Albert was very disturbed and
finally offered, as compensation, the fact that he had, after

all, chosen this man's café for his party, and that too was a form of recognition of friendship. Just as the first incident—the standard morning-after greeting—affirms the privacy of emotional friendship, so this one demonstrates the danger and impropriety of conducting such friendship in the public sphere.

15. Special-Purpose Groups

There are a number of special-purpose groups in the valley, most of them restricted, by tradition, to male membership but some open to and, in fact, dominated by women—the Red Cross, for instance, and the Society of Ancient Costumes. Men may participate in the valley-wide political parties, in service societies such as the Samaritains (a first-aid society) or the Brancardiers ("stretcher-bearers" who assist invalids on the annual pilgrimage to Lourdes), in the society of *patoisants* (a group devoted to preserving and encouraging the local patois), and others. Young people of both sexes participate, separately, in church-sponsored youth activities such as Scouts and various small groups devoted to special interests or study (a cinema club, a reading circle, an outing club). One village has organized a Societé de Tir (shooting society) open to the valley—a very popular activity in other parts of Switzerland, but appealing only to a small group in Bagnes, none of them Brusonins. Another valley-wide organization which has no known members in Bruson is the Croix d'Or—a society with a formal membership list of pledged teetotalers.

Many of the individual villages have local versions of some of these valley-wide activities—a Jeunesse Catholique (the militant Catholic youth organization) or a section of one or both of the major political parties. In addition, an individual

128

village may have an independent singing society—which is, in several cases, a mixed chorus—as well as its own economic cooperatives. At the village level, these associations are unique and distinct, even when supported by the larger valley-wide organization.

In Bruson there are four kinds of voluntary associations: a Jeunesse group, a singing society, a political *cercle* for each of the two major parties, and several economic cooperatives. These special-purpose groups can be distinguished broadly in terms of the nature of membership. In the first three, membership is on an individual basis, the member representing only himself, while in the economic cooperatives the members are *ménages*, each of which is treated as a unit with respect to formal participation. This is in keeping with the essentially economic nature of the ménage.

Using this basic dichotomy of individual versus ménage membership, one can further distinguish these two types of special-purpose groups. Membership in the economic associations is limited to participants in the particular economic activity—a ménage with no livestock cannot be a member of the *laiterie*—but it is not restricted by any other criteria such as sex, age, or marital status. The *chef de l'exploitation*—the nominal head of the ménage—is entitled to membership, whether this person is a woman, or a bachelor living alone, or the adult unmarried son of a widow. Membership in the cooperative is inherited, but a new membership may be purchased after petitioning the society. Each member—that is, an individual representing a ménage—is entitled to one vote, and that vote may be cast by any person in the ménage, man, woman, or child.

Although there are no formal criteria for joining any of the special-purpose groups based on individual membership, certain informal criteria actually operate—namely, age, sex, and marital status. Only in the Jeunesse is sex a formal criterion, restricting membership to men. Effectively, then, only men participate in the Jeunesse of Bruson, as well as in the singing society and in the political cercles.

Alpenrose, the singing society, has been at various times in its history a mixed chorus, and members today do not preclude the possibility of including women. Women, however, show no

interest in participating, and, in fact, it would be difficult to
transform the group into a mixed chorus once again, given the
nature of part-singing. There would have to be an immediate
introduction of several women—enough to provide personnel
for the Soprano and Alto parts in sufficient number to balance
the male sections of Tenor and Bass. Aside from the difficulty
of meeting musical requirements, however, the group has
evolved into one characterized by male behavior—for instance,
drinking communally from a bottle of wine during rehearsal
breaks—and the introduction of women would place constraints
on these patterns. Membership, then, is open to any man
interested in group singing. Members pay a small annual fee
to defray the expenses of the group—chiefly for music and
wine—and each member is entitled to vote.

The political cercles are part of the larger party organizations
of the valley. Again, while there are no official restrictions with
respect to age, sex, or marital status, the participation of women
is simply not countenanced. And, as in the case of Alpenrose,
women respond by showing no interest in the activity. The
cercles have no membership lists, and their meetings are publi-
cized and open to any interested men. Anyone attending a
meeting is entitled to vote, even if he is known to be an adherent
of the other party. Office-holding is restricted to local residents
(of Bruson and Le Sappey), regardless of their origin or *bourgeoisie*. It is also informally limited to eligible voters in the
larger polity—that is, men of twenty years of age or older.

Members of the Jeunesse are assumed to be young and
unmarried, though still of marriageable age. Although *jeunes
gens* (young men) denotes men of the age group immediately
following childhood—those who have completed compulsory
education or, in some cases, only primary education—the informal stipulation of bachelorhood extends this age group to
include men in their thirties. Thus, members of the Jeunesse,
while all unmarried, may range in age from about thirteen to
about forty. Effectively, the group consists of men in their late
teens and twenties, since those who are younger or older have
other interests and other possibilities for association.

While Alpenrose and the political cercles have no age or
marital status criteria, they are quite distinct in composition
with respect to these two variables. In a sample group of

twenty-one Alpenrose "regulars"—representing two-thirds of
the nominal membership—the median age was twenty-seven
years, with a range of fifteen to seventy-five. Twelve individuals
(57 percent) were under thirty, and six more (29 percent)
between thirty and fifty. In this group, fifteen individuals (71
percent) were unmarried.

For comparison with this group, I used a sample of the
membership of the Conservative Party cercle. While this political party, officially called Democrate-Chrétien-Social, has a
two-thirds majority in the valley at large over the other major
party, the Radical-Socialiste, in the Bruson-Sappey sections
their numbers are approximately equal—about sixty men belong
to each party. The sample chosen was based on the attendance
at a meeting of the Conservative Party cercle. Nineteen men
were present, representing about one-third of the total cercle
membership and including most of its active personnel. The
median age was thirty-eight years, with a range of twenty-five
to seventy-five. Only two men were under thirty—about 10
percent, compared with 71 percent in the Alpenrose sample.
The age group thirty-fifty consisted of twelve individuals—63
percent, compared with 29 percent in the Alpenrose sample.
Only seven men were unmarried—32 percent, compared with
71 percent in the Alpenrose sample.

AGE

	Under 30	Over 30
Alpenrose	12	9
cercle	2	17

MARITAL STATUS

	Married	Unmarried
Alpenrose	6	15
cercle	12	7

In these two samples of about the same total size, there is
a striking difference in median age—twenty-seven years in
Alpenrose, and thirty-eight years in the Conservative Party

cercle—and there are twice as many unmarried men in Alpenrose as in the cercle. Because of the difference in age range,
however, certain adjustments must be made to compare marital
status in the two groups. To begin with, the comparison should
be confined to the age group twenty-five to sixty-four, since
this exists in both groups and excludes only one older individual
in both. This restriction also takes into account the rarity of
marriage for men under twenty-five, the average age being
twenty-nine. In the village as a whole, thirty-two men (46
percent) in the age group twenty-five to sixty-four are unmarried. In the Alpenrose sample, six (50 percent) in this age group
are unmarried, and, in the cercle sample, seven (39 percent)
are unmarried. While the Alpenrose sample shows a higher
proportion of unmarried men between twenty-five and sixty-
four than does the village population, this proportion is lower
in the cercle sample.

One is, thus, justified in describing the political cercle as
consisting of older men, more of whom are married, than is
the case in Alpenrose. Age and marital status are, clearly,
functional correlates of membership in these groups. One can
now place these two groups on a continuum, preceded by the
Jeunesse and followed by the economic cooperatives, with
respect to these criteria. The Jeunesse is the youngest group
and consists entirely of unmarried men; the men of Alpenrose
are somewhat older, mostly in their twenties and thirties, and
about a third of them are married; the men of the Conservative
cercle are still older, in their thirties and forties, and two-thirds
are married; finally, members of the economic cooperatives are
not individuals at all but ménage units—implying marriage, in
most cases, and property ownership, but encompassing a wide
range of ages.

Having established this continuum based on the demographic
characteristics of members, let us now consider differences
among the groups with respect to organization and leadership.
Membership criteria and types are correlated with what may
be called the "seriousness" of the group. The economic cooperative—based on formal membership not restricted by age, sex,
or marital status but limited to ménage units—are vitally tied
to the livelihood of the village, and their purposes are very
limited and specific. The laiterie association offers cooperative

facilities for processing and marketing milk products; the *consortages* provide for their members summer grazing land in the high pastures—which, though bourgeoisie property, is held in usufruct for ninety-nine years by the consortage; the fruit and vegetable syndicate offers cooperative marketing of the cash crops (strawberries and raspberries) as well as cooperative pesticide treatment for all crops.

These special-purpose groups meet regularly but very infrequently—perhaps two or three times a year—for the sole purpose of carrying out their objectives. Leadership is supplied by a Committee, usually of three people, headed by a President and including a Secretary who handles minutes, financial records, and various correspondence. The Secretary is elected for a three-year term but usually serves reluctantly for several successive terms. The other two members of the Committee are elected for three-year terms, staggered between them. The election of these two Committee members is usually a purely nominal one, since the new member is *"le plus fort producteur"* —the individual (*chef de l'exploitation*) whose yield in that particular area (milk or market crops) has been the highest in the past year among those who have not already served on the Committee. Because of the manner of choice, no prestige is attached to such office-holding in the economic cooperatives since prior officers will probably have surpassed his production. Thus, leadership is completely divorced from political activity and completely tied to the stated area of interest of the group.

In contrast to this "plus fort producteur" principle, the other voluntary associations choose their leaders on the basis of assumed merit, competence, popularity, and willingness to serve—that is, the choice is a political one. Another basic criterion for leadership in these groups is youth. This criterion is associated with a feeling that younger men should be given preference over older ones for opportunities to distinguish themselves and to do public service. The President of Alpenrose is twenty-one years old, while the median age of the sample is twenty-seven years; the President of the Conservative cercle is thirty-eight years old and the median age of the six-man governing Committee is thirty-two, while the median age of the sample is thirty-eight.

As the "seriousness" of group purpose diminishes, criteria

for leadership become more political in nature, more diffuse, and less directly associated with the avowed purpose of the group. The President of Alpenrose is neither the best singer nor the musical director, and the President of the cercle is neither the most astute politician nor the village *conseiller*. Seriousness of group purpose is determined in part by specificity. For instance, the laiterie is a serious organization not only because it impinges directly on livelihood but also because its purpose is simply and specifically to optimize milk processing and marketing. The purpose of the cercle, however, cannot be so easily and directly stated. It is, in fact, manifold and includes the support of the valley-wide party organization, the furthering of the local interests of the cercle within the larger organization, and the opportunity for members to air their political views within the relative privacy of the village kinship-friendship network.

The stated purposes of Alpenrose are to satisfy its members' love of singing and to *cultiver l'amitié* (cultivate friendship) among them. Alpenrose meets regularly and frequently for rehearsal—twice a week during the "dead season" of December to May—and also organizes outings for its members, either to sing as a group in another village or for a purely recreational purpose such as a *souper* or a picnic lunch in the *mayens*.

Associated with decreasing seriousness of group purpose, then, are more frequent meetings, looser group structure, a generally younger population with a larger proportion of unmarried men, and leadership based on youth, popularity, and willingness. As the group purpose becomes more diffuse, one also observes the appearance of sodality-like symbols of identity and unity—a group name, a flag, a uniform for members, and accounts of group origin. This constellation is present in Alpenrose and in the Jeunesse. These two groups are also assigned collective personality traits by the village as a whole: the Jeunesse, while young and unruly, always behaves correctly as a group, whereas Alpenrose is known for making trouble and having difficulties when it functions as a group outside the village.

These attributions of personality to the two groups are particularly interesting when one realizes that, of the two, only Alpenrose has any formal organization. The Jeunesse seems to be merged with the age grade it represents. It has no formal leadership and no activities or meetings outside of those traditionally assigned to it in connection with the patron-saint day, when the group is responsible for performing as the Army of St. Michel and for organizing the public dance. Nevertheless, both Alpenrose and the Jeunesse project public images—of which they are well aware—and there is a friendly rivalry between them even though there is a considerable overlap in membership.

This concept of group image recalls the public image of the village as a whole with respect to the outside world. The two, however, are never confused, and each special-purpose group must stand or fall on its own merits with neither support from the village of which it is a part nor the power to influence the reputation of the village. The special-purpose group, while providing a service for villagers, exists on a different level of organization from the village unit. In the same way, the group is not responsible to its individual members for its collective functioning or personality. Individual members are, however, responsible to the group, since they have agreed to give up a certain amount of personal freedom for the benefit of the collectivity.

The principle is well illustrated in an incident involving Alpenrose. The group had been invited to sing in another village in connection with a public event. After the performance, the singers went to a local café where four of them became very drunk, abusive, and destructive. This incident, occurring outside Bruson, gave rise to disapproving comments by non-Brusonins referring to the group image of Alpenrose: "Those people always cause trouble." A few days later, the President of Alpenrose called a meeting in Bruson at which the incident was discussed. Everyone knew which individuals were guilty of misbehavior, but the major part of the discussion centered on the distinction between group and individual behavior.

Two principles of behavior were explicitly stated. The first was a recognition that Alpenrose members were also Brusonins and, thus, were expected to act in accordance with the public image of Brusonin men: to *boire un verre* with their fellows. A finer interpretation of this behavioral guideline, however, is the expectation that a Brusonin knows when to stop drinking

—an expectation which was not fulfilled in the present circumstance. The second principle of behavior referred to the Brusonin as a member of a society and, specifically, to his obligation
to that society. On the occasion of a group-sponsored excursion,
a member was expected to behave *en societé* and not as an
individuel, since outsiders would regard him as a member of
the group and his good or bad behavior would be attributed
to the group as a whole.

This discussion was actually an exercise in group solidarity.
Individual behavior—misbehavior in this case—was acknowledged and chastised but deemphasized in favor of the unity
of the society. Reference was made to the forty-seven years
of society existence, and to the fact that "this was the first
time such a thing had happened," that the society had always
been known for its *correcte* behavior. The conductor—a Brusonin who married in Le Châble and comes to Bruson twice
weekly for rehearsals—was cited for his *dévouement* (devotion).
One of the founders of the society—a seventy-five-year-old man
who was born in another village but has lived in Bruson since
childhood—was gratefully acknowledged as the *doyen* of the
society, a sort of figurehead representing its good reputation.
One of the older members reminded the group of its objectives:
"cultiver l'amitié entre nous et apporter de la gaieté aux autres"
("to cultivate friendship among us and to bring gaiety to
others"). The discussion, then, was dominated by symbols of
group unity: its origin, its founding culture-heroes, the devotion
of its leaders, its fine reputation (a self-image which contradicts
the public image), and its basic objectives which, in fact,
transcend the special purpose of the group and spill over into
the more binding area of friendship.

By way of sharp contrast, such a situation would be impossible in one of the economic cooperatives where the purpose of
the group is simple, unitary, and specific and where the group
organization is correspondingly tight and functional. The
"seriousness" of purpose of the cooperatives is enough justification for their existence and solidarity. There is no need for
symbols of unity or expressions of solidarity. The group exists
only for its members. Should an individual decide it was no
longer to his advantage to be a member—if, for instance, he
sold his livestock—he would simply withdraw, taking with him

his fair share of profits for his term of membership. The group would have no need of and no desire for his continued participation. If all Brusonins gave up their livestock, the laiterie and the consortages would simply cease to exist.

A society like Alpenrose, however, acquires an existence apart from its individual members. The benefits accrued from membership are as diffuse and unspecifiable as the purpose of the group and vary from one member to another. The basis for group existence, therefore, must be sought in a region where all members are in agreement: the region of friendship. Because of the size of the group, one understands this to be the kind of instrumental friendship that is said to exist among all villagers. The affective atmosphere is one of friendliness, and the bonding material is tradition.

Although the group has a history and tradition separate from that of the village, similar elements appear in both. The original founders of Alpenrose are held up as models of behavior; the traditional occupation of the society is group-singing; this common interest is supported by the conviviality associated with drinking wine; a large proportion of the group is related through actual kinship; and there is a tradition of fathers introducing their sons into the group. In the sample of twenty-one individuals, fifteen ménages were represented of which five had two representatives each: two of these were father and son, and three were pairs of unmarried brothers. In addition to these five pairs of co-resident relatives, there were three pairs of brothers living in separate ménages. Thus, of the twenty-one individuals in the sample, fourteen (66 percent) had at least one close kinsman in the group.

This high frequency of actual kinship ties among group members simulates the situation in the village as a whole: "Since most of us are related, and since friendship (friendliness) is most often associated with kinship, then we are a group of friends." Because there is a certain rate of turn-over in membership, particularly among the younger unmarried men, a great many Brusonins have, at one time or another, been members of Alpenrose. The fact that this special-purpose group draws its members randomly and exclusively from the larger village group does not make it representative of the village. The association, however, with this village group of great

stability and solidarity provides the context and the mechanisms for solidarity in the special-purpose group.

Alpenrose—unlike the economic cooperatives—is solidary in
an organic sense: its cohesion is not based on the likeness of
interests of its members but rather on their relationships to
one another and to the group as a whole. The very success
of Alpenrose depends on this blending of kinship, friendship,
and voluntary association. Thus, its apparent weakness, with
respect to seriousness of purpose or tightness of organization,
is transformed into a strength, and its members, while giving
up more personal freedom than they do in an economic cooperative, also gain more from the association.

Part IV

Individual and Community

16. The Ideology of Uniqueness

In Part III, I presented the Brusonin as a member of various groups—familistic, affective, economic, political, religious, and recreational. Although such a study reveals information both about the individual and about the community as a whole, my point of view has been essentially social-structural. Before considering wider implications, I will examine the matter from within, from the vantage point of an individual member of the society.

A Brusonin can be identified and described by a number of basic attributes. Some are associated with him from birth and remain fixed through his life—sex, family name (for a man), political affiliation. Another—age—changes in a regular way beyond his control. Still others are subject to some individual control—marital status and occupation.

Since every individual possesses all these attributes, one could assume that the list of attributes constitutes a standard for identification, measurement, and comparison of Brusonins. The attributes making up a list of variables common to all members of the population could then be used to draw a

description of the population itself. This description would take
the form of a demographic analysis in terms of age, sex, and
marital status with supplementary pictures of occupational
structure, political affiliation, and the distribution of family
names with respect to all of these.

The interpretation of this analysis, however, turns out to
yield no information that was not readily available by direct
inquiry. Any Brusonin could tell the investigator: that the
proportion of men to women is about equal except in the age
group twenty to forty-five, where men outnumber women; that
there is a high proportion of unmarried men in the village;
that a few family names dominate the population; that there
are somewhat more Radicals in Bruson than in Bagnes generally; that most Brusonins are *paysan-ouvriers* or have *métiers*,
but that more of them still practice agriculture than do the
inhabitants of other villages.

These basic attributes—age, sex, marital status, family name,
political affiliation, and occupation—though necessary, are not
sufficient for a meaningful anthropological description of a
Brusonin or of the community as a whole. Each attribute
carries a host of implications, some of which can be inferred
directly from the attribute and others that reveal large areas
of variability which depend on individual choice.

Age strongly implies *classe*—an ascribed status which groups
all Bagnards born in the same year. If a Brusonin is asked
(by an outsider who does not know better) *"Quel âge avez-
vous?"* ("How old are you?") he will reply—*"Je suis de '33."*
("I am of [born in] '33."). He will refer to his companion thus:
"Il est de ma classe." ("He is of my classe.") In these cases,
when asked for an individual identification, he responds by
citing a group membership. He is born into this group, but
the group does not begin to function until the time of First
Communion—at about age thirteen. From then on, the group
reaffirms its existence through regular planned activities—an
annual *sortie de classe* (a two- or three-day excursion to some
place of interest) or more frequent *soupers* (suppers). Although
some classes are known to be more active than others in this
respect, one's classe membership does not depend on participation. Classe membership completely replaces age identification. In all official documents, for instance—lists of voters,

income tax returns, land purchase papers—the individual's name is always followed by his classe membership, the year of his birth.

Age-grades are also directly inferred from the age attribute, but they are informal groupings and exist only until adulthood —twenty years, when a man becomes eligible to vote (women since 1970) and enters military service. The age-grade *les enfants* (children) is characterized by age and occupation. It includes children between seven and thirteen—primary school *écoliers* (school children)—and those from thirteen to sixteen who are *étudiants* (students) in Collège (secondary school) or *école ménagère* (school of home economics). Those men who have completed compulsory education but have not yet attained adulthood are referred to as *les jeunes* (the young).

In many ways, these individuals, at various stages of pre-adulthood, form a separate subculture. Although still dependent economically, they have great social freedom. The society groups them into age-grades which actually protect their individuality. Since these individuals are not considered members of the larger village structure, they are not concerned with the preservation of their equal status in the community. Because of their economic dependence, debt and reciprocity have no meaning for them, and they need not exploit the instrumental friendship network of the village. Their freedom is best expressed in the emotional friendships which they form and readily admit.

The immediately pre-adult age-grade produces the first significant collision between the two variables of age and sex. While the boys of les jeunes begin to participate in the more loosely-organized special-purpose groups—the Jeunesse and Alpenrose —the girls begin to disappear into the *ménage*. Sexual distinctions define certain general areas of labor—housework and child-rearing for women, and the heavy agricultural chores such as bringing in hay for men. The essential significance of sex, however, is that it clearly defines arenas of social participation. The first broad division is in terms of public and private activity. The ménage, the essence of private life, is the woman's territory: the dwelling, the barn and other agricultural outbuildings, and the ménage lands. Her place is in the *foyer*—a word meaning "hearth" in standard French and derived from *feu*, or fire. In patois and in local French usage, "feu" is interchangeable with "ménage"—recalling that the ménage is not only a private domain of female activity but that it is defined by gastronomic exclusivity. The linguistic identification of kitchen and ménage reiterates the ideological identification of woman and private arena.

Men participate in the public arena—the café, the *laiterie*, voluntary associations throughout the valley, métiers which remove them daily from the village. But the collision at adulthood between age and sex does not stop at the definition of separate arenas of participation. Women continue to participate in classe activities, and they do so as individuals—not as daughters or wives or mothers. Since marriage between members of the same classe is uncommon, the attribute of age, in this situation, supersedes that of sex: men or women, as a matter of course, go on classe outings without their mates.

Another implication of sex has to do with piety as expressed in religious observance. It is said that women are more pious than men—a belief easily confirmed by counting the men and the women at Mass. This relationship between sex and piety, however, is contradicted by the relationship between political affiliation and piety: broadly speaking, Conservatives are church-goers, and Radicals are anti-clerical. Clearly, then, religious observance is not restricted to women, and the category of sex provides insufficient information.

Family name is a similarly insufficient category. One can identify a man as a Maret, and can discuss the *famille* Maret at great length. One cannot, however, use this information to describe the individual except in terms of his political affiliation. His famille membership will tell us whether he is a Conservative or a Radical, and from this one can deduce his religious beliefs. If, however, he treats his wife badly, making her work "like a servant," one can neither refer to his famille for explanation nor attribute the quality of "treating one's wife badly" to all Marets. One may, with propriety, attack the individual—since this kind of behavior is within his control—but one makes the attack on an individual, a man responsible for his action, and not on his famille.

Although an individual's family name yields little personal information about him and is, in turn, impervious to his own

behavior, a man can be identified very well through his nickname. This is almost always a name of reference rather than
of address. Nicknames either describe their bearers or distinguish them from others of the same given name—by citing
quartier residence (Célina de la Fontaine), father's name (Louis
de Candide), husband's name (Marcelle de Roland), wife's
mother's name (Louis de Rose), present or past occupation (*le
cantonnier, le Président*), a particular incident (Maurice de
la Guerre), a religious attitude (*le capucin*), a personality (*la
terreur*), or a physical feature (*le barbu*). Insofar as nicknames
label reputations, Bruson stands as a perfect example of the
following dictum: "Membership of a community does not
depend upon having a *good* reputation: only upon having a
reputation" (Bailey 1971:7).

The prevalence of nicknames, with their functions of description and distinction, suggests that Brusonins themselves identify individuals in two ways: Who is he? and Which one is
he? The answers to these questions depend on a system of
classification different from ours. Some of the categories in the
Brusonin system refer to basic attributes. The classes *vieux
garçon* (bachelor) and *vieille fille* (spinster), for instance, refer
to our variables of marital status and age. The information
given, however, is the speaker's attitude of scorn mixed with
pity for "unmarried people past marriageable age." The class
pratiquant (religiously observant) refers to sex and political
affiliation but singles out an extreme of religious behavior.

Another class, *progressiste* (progressive), has little to do with
political affiliation, as one might expect it did, for most men
think of themselves as progressiste. The context here is the
Brusonin's perception of the future of his village. One is reminded of his use of the word "folklore" to describe things
old-fashioned and insignificant. More information is supplied
by the negative counterpart of this class, expressed in the
phrase *ceux qui disent toujours Non* (those who always say
No). Individuals in this class "said No" to the purchase of
mayen land in the 1930s to expand the *alpages*; in 1968 they
"said No" to the sale of that same mayen land for touristic
development.

A number of other Brusonin categories, even further removed
from our set of basic attributes, refer to individual interests

and personality traits: the readers (a class of about six members who are known to like reading); the *instruits* (those with formal education beyond that required by the canton, or who have taught themselves certain skills thought to be intellectual, such as languages); the *travailleuses* (a few women who work "like men" in intensity); those who "never go to the café" (a very small class, thus yielding much information about its members); those who are *méchant* (mean) when drunk (a rather large class).

Categories such as these are frequently used by Brusonins to distinguish their fellows. The Brusonin classification system differs in many important ways from our system of basic attributes. The classes do not account for all individuals. Their membership is variable, depending on the context and on the speaker. They refer to a wide range of behavior, beliefs, and attitudes as well as to certain of the basic attributes such as age and sex and to specific areas of the culture—economy, religion, social organization. Some classes are very small, while others encompass almost the entire village. Nicknames are also part of this classification scheme, though each category contains only a single member.

If the Brusonin classification system seems disorganized to us, it is because its function is not to lump individuals together but to single them out. The collisions and contradictions which appeared in our set of basic attributes are not properties of the culture but of our system of classification. The value of the basic attributes system is its exposure of the Brusonin's own conception of the dichotomy between individual and community.

The unity of the village—its peasant tradition and all the ramifications thereof—requires and supports individual uniqueness. Brusonins are not interchangeable parts in a mechanical system. Each one works in a micro-environment to which he must constantly be adapting. He is a generalist equipped with a varied stock of resources and techniques. One of his resources is uniqueness: a particular plot of strawberries that has been producing for twenty years (instead of the typical four or five); an unneeded mayen which he exchanges with his brother for some *vignes*; the old bedroom of a married son which he rents to skiers. One of his techniques is self-submer-

sion: his participation in the Syndicate of Fruits and Vegetables, his presence at a *souper de la fin d'année*, his service
on the laiterie Committee as *le plus fort producteur*.

The successful Brusonin is always playing off his uniqueness
against his sameness. When I speak of Bruson as an egalitatian
society, I am referring to this quality of sameness—founded
not on absolute equality but on an estimate of equivalence.
The basis for equivalence is the common heritage—a vocation,
a genealogy, a personality—or what a Brusonin means when
he says: *"Ici nous sommes tous égaux"* ("Here we are all the
same"). There are no *riches* (but some are more *aisés*, or
comfortable); no one is more intelligent (but some are more
instruits); no one is more pious (but some are more *prati-
quants*). These categories which he uses to describe his fellows
consist of exceptions, and implicit in this classification system
is the identification of individual uniqueness.

The grouping of individuals according to their unique qualities—even to the point of recognizing one-member categories
(nicknames)—is not different in kind but only in degree
from the social-structural groupings I discussed in the previous
chapter. One may visualize a spectrum of devices for identifying
individuals. At one end of the spectrum—the one most strongly
associated with community—an individual's unique identity is
completely submerged in his village membership. He is identified as a Brusonin, a member of a common-descent group whose
traditions come from the *ancêtres*. Further along on the spectrum, the individual is more specifically identified as a member
of a famille with a name, a political affiliation, and a religious
attitude. This description is further narrowed at that point
on the spectrum when genealogical memory begins and an
ancêtre becomes a known lineal antecedent. Now the individual
can be identified as a member of a particular *parenté* and the
ménage with which it is associated.

At this point, the spectrum shimmers with a wealth of
information. The individual as ménage member is a *chef de
l'exploitation*. As such, he controls a particular property base
consisting of his own and his wife's inheritance, modified and
improved through his own resources and abilities. By virtue
of being a property owner, he participates in an economic
cooperative. As a married man, he is a member of a political

cercle and perhaps also of other special-interest groups. He
and his wife both engage in various kinds of social activities—his
being in the public sphere of the café and his wife's in the
private sphere of the ménage. In addition to having access to
the instrumental friendship network associated with the village
as a whole, he has private relationships with "best friends"
and "good friends" which are not subject to external regulation.
At this point on the spectrum, the individual has established
his claims to independence and equal standing in the "one
family" of the village. Now he can be described more precisely
by citing his unique qualities, and finally—through his nickname which refers explicitly to his uniqueness—he is identified
as an individual.

The end-points of the spectrum of group membership refer
directly to the dichotomy of individual and community. The
Brusonin is identified, at one extreme, by his anonymous
membership in the village and, at the other, by his membership
in a group characterized by uniqueness. The village of Bruson,
therefore, can be described as a unified whole composed of
diverse elements.

Although the ménage is the minimal unit in the social
structure, its greatest significance rests on its function as a
dramatic vehicle for individual expression. The ménage is
opposed structurally to the "one family" of the village. The
individual mediates this relation, exploiting the structure to
his greatest personal advantage by moving between the two
poles. He benefits fully from membership in a small tightly-knit
community, without giving up his standing in it as an equal
member, through the use of a simple system of reciprocity.
Every service rendered is paid for in a currency accessible to
all—the ménage currency of food and drink.

The currency of reciprocity reflects the peasant ideology of
freedom through private ownership. Ideally, the food and drink
offered as payment are the products of one's own land and
labor. Although the Brusonin does not aspire to rapid and easy
expansion of his capital investments or to a high level of
profit-taking, he is, in effect, a capitalist operating in a free-en-
terprise system. He seeks to reinvest his profits and to maintain
good public relations. In the optimal condition, he preserves
the value of his capital and liquidates immediately any debts

incurred. When this state is achieved, the peasant ideology is satisfied: the Brusonin is free, independent, and self-sustaining.

Villagers are not rivals but colleagues in this enterprise. As such, all are part of a larger system—the village community—which actually depends for its existence on the consent of its members to abide by the rules they have established. The rules of reciprocity are based on the traditional pre-monetary culture which prescribes "payment" (in food or drink) for men and "replacement" (in produce or labor) for women—the objective on both sides being to annul debt and restore the participants to a state of equivalence.

Two object lessons—either of which might easily have turned into a methodological blunder—dramatized the essentially traditional nature of this system. I was visiting a couple and told the wife that her husband had kindly "bought" me a cup of coffee in the café the day before. The husband looked thunderstruck, and I realized I had said something improper. I immediately corrected the word "bought" to "offered"—emphasizing the gift aspect of the event and removing it from the monetary context—and he relaxed. He went on to tell his wife admiringly that I had even refused to take cream in the coffee (at an extra charge of ten *centimes*)—implying that I was a good Brusonin, capable of freely accepting a gift while stubbornly refusing to accept too great a gift and thus put myself in a position of debt.

The second incident arose when a woman heard I had been helping others pick raspberries and offered me a job working in her own harvest. By offering monetary payment, she was treating me as a non-villager—specifically, as one of the agricultural workers who are hired by a few households to assist in the harvest. I refused in confusion and said that I would be glad to give her a little help, but not for money. She quickly reassessed the situation and invited me to come along and simply pick some raspberries for myself. To this I agreed, but I was careful to keep only a small part of the berries I had picked. My action transformed the situation into a standard village event of service and payment. We now stood in a potential employer-employee relationship, and I was immediately invited to tea in denial of the commercial context.

The ménage in its relationship with the converging family

is the locus of property ownership, the foundation of the peasant ideology of freedom. The ménage is, in fact, perceived as an economic rather than a kinship unit. In its early history, it is economically dependent on the two parent ménages, which still control the property. Gradually, however, the new ménage takes ascendance, and—when the property is divided among the heirs—the *chef de famille* becomes the chef de l'exploitation. Since property is inherited equally and bilaterally, the economic base and success of the ménage depend on the mutual goodwill of its founders, the married couple. Swiss law requires that they consider their separate properties as a single unit. But, since the children will also inherit equally and bilaterally, the property base of the ménage has a life-span of only one generation, and success depends on the astuteness with which it is manipulated and developed by the chef de l'exploitation.

Manipulation of the property base, though individualistic, is not competitive among Brusonins. There is, however, potential competition for limited resources among the group of heirs at the moment of *partage*. Although *chicanes* arise frequently from inheritance disputes, competition is not encouraged and every attempt is made to accommodate personal needs. When perfect accommodation is impossible, the chicane itself—by closing avenues of communication between the individuals involved—puts an end to competition. Competition is absent in the larger village community as well. An individual's ultimate success is perceived to depend on his discriminating acquisition of resources to supplement his inheritance and his skillful manipulation of this property base.

The Brusonin is a free and independent agent with a unique set of multiple resources who asserts his freedom by giving up some of it to participate in the village community. He thereby benefits from sharing in the self-image of the village as a collectivity with a common history and tradition, language, vocation, personality, and continuity. A unique individual, he is a member of a common-descent group ("here we are all related") and has access to a mutual-aid network based on instrumental friendship ("here we are all friendly"). The loss of freedom is a direct result of this participation, which places one's dealings with family, friends, and associates in the public eye and subject to public regulation. In compensation, the

Brusonin reserves for himself a private and independent sphere of activity—in the ménage and in his emotional friendships.

The co-existence of instrumental and emotional forms of friendship is not a contradiction but rather a special case of Wolf's (1966a) argument. Following his reasoning, one expects to find emotional friendship in societies of low social mobility where individuals are dependent on a highly structured and closed social system based on kinship. In such societies, emotional friendship may offer the only outlet for "emotional release and catharsis from the strains and pressures of role-playing" (Wolf 1966a:11). Instrumental friendship, on the other hand, is associated with situations of high mobility, a loosely structured kinship system, and a nonegalitarian network of influence which the individual can exploit by making the right connections.

Working from my paradigmatic separation of individual and community, one may describe Bruson as an economically individualistic society based on an egalitarian ideology. Equivalence is ascribed to all Brusonins by virtue of a common heritage founded on the peasant vocation with its ideology of freedom based on property ownership. To claim equal standing by virtue of this common heritage, then, means to be independent and free of debt. The village-wide instrumental friendship network, built on the actual or imputed kinship of all members, is the egalitarian structure which assures individual independence, providing mechanisms for correcting momentary imbalances that result from debt situations.

Instrumental friendship pervades the social life of Bruson and contributes heavily to the cultural continuity of the village. In a sense, instrumental friendship *is* the social system of Bruson, for it is equated with the village-wide kinship network which ascribes equivalence to all Brusonins. Among Brusonins, there is competition neither to surpass in resources nor to excel in their manipulation—property and its management belonging to the private sphere of the ménage. Yet, a high value is placed on presentation as an *equal* member of the society, an individual whose privacy is to be respected. Through instrumental friendship behavior, the Brusonin displays his equality and preserves his privacy. His emotional friendships, then, are in direct response to the pressures placed on him in public behavior. "Best friends," like property and ménage, are private. Their identities and the conduct of these relationships—like the manipulation of ménage property—are not subject to external regulation but depend entirely on the individual, his resources and management methods.

The continuous interplay between individual and community in Bruson is expressed social-structurally in terms of the ménage and its property base, the village-wide kinship system, the instrumental friendship network, and the private and individually regulated emotional friendships. The ideological opposition of sameness and uniqueness supports this structure and permits individuals to act independently or to ally themselves with the village collectivity. The sum of individual uniqueness is a culture based on the interdependence of diverse elements and whose survival rests on the preservation of diversity.

17. The "Little Community"

I have made a minute examination of a few selected features of a single tiny village in one of the "small nations" of Europe. I must now step back to consider certain larger questions that have emerged—for example: Are these people indeed peasants? Am I, in fact, talking about a peasant village, about the peasantry level of socio-cultural integration? Or should I think of it as a question at all?

Definitions, identifications, and typologies are but stepping-stones in the stream of knowledge. Why label a certain society as "primitive" or "peasant" or "modern"? First of all, this effort facilitates analysis, through such variables as degree of societal autonomy, or the relative importance of kinship, or the locus of property ownership. These operations depend on useful generalizations distilled from earlier ethnographic studies. I am, with my own data, putting the generalizations to yet another test. If they work, I use them—and increase my confidence in them. If they do not work, I face a problem—which to discard, generalizations or data? In fact, I do neither. Instead, I ask: why does this generalization fail to "work on"—that is, fail to explain—my own data?

In either case, success or failure to explain, the label or "law" is a convenient tool for talking about the data. Consider the

title of a paper by Lloyd Fallers—"Are African Cultivators to
Be Called 'Peasants'?" (1961). Beneath, its apparent naiveté
is a sophisticated question: what can one learn about peasants
by trying out the definition on *this* society? It is this question
I wish to ask about Bruson.

All current definitions of peasantry still draw heavily on
those framed by Kroeber in 1948 and by Redfield in the
succeeding decade. Our understanding of peasantry today rests
on the fundamental principles that peasantries are "part-societies with part-cultures" (Kroeber 1948), that the part-whole
relationship reflects the interplay between Great and Little
Traditions (Redfield and Singer 1954), and that the characteristics of any particular peasant society are summarized in
the concept of the "little community" (Redfield 1956). The
"little community" is distinctive, small, homogeneous, self-sufficient (Redfield 1956:4), and, by implication, closed.

Redfield's description applies to an ideal type, conceived at
a time when ethnographic data on peasantry were scarce. We
know from the study of biological populations that every real
community is to some extent open—subject to some forces in
its cultural and physical environment. For this reason, a community must have a store of adaptive mechanisms which permit
it to enjoy the occasional sunshine and to weather the occasional storm.

Accumulating ethnographic evidence suggests that peasant
societies in Europe have *never* been closed. As adaptive social
systems, all such societies have contained a wealth of regulatory
mechanisms, direct outgrowths of the society's contact with
its environment. Regulation of that environment may involve
manipulation of features of the larger society, of the Great
Tradition. It may even, in the extreme case, require closure
of the peasant community. Short of this extreme, however,
peasantries are characterized by population movement in and
out of the community. Before examining adaptive strategies
that reveal the openness of the "little community," one must
consider the problem of identifying and delimiting the peasant
community itself.

Geertz has written that in Bali the peasant "community"
is not a fixed social unit, but rather "a compound of social
structures . . . the intersection of theoretically separable planes

of social organization" (Geertz 1959:256). One must speak instead of "communities" based on temple membership, common residence, irrigation societies, the "title system" of ascribed social status, kinship ties, voluntary organizations, and legal administration.

Even where villages were clearly distinguishable, as in traditional China, Skinner (1964) noted that the "effective social field" of the Chinese peasant was "not the village but the standard marketing community" encompassing eighteen villages. This "community"—a "culture-bearing unit"—was defined economically but also served important social, religious, and political functions. Within the standard marketing community, the peasant was able to satisfy most of his needs— for goods and services, for credit, for recreation, for finding a daughter-in-law, for meeting his occupational associates.

Working in the Swiss Alps, I too had difficulty with the notion of "little community." Bruson, after all, is one of a number of villages in a larger cultural unit—the commune—which has been exposed to increasingly intensive contact with the outside world for the past forty years. Yet in spite of the obvious failure to meet Redfield's criterion of self-sufficiency, Bruson seems to have all the other features of the "little community." It is small, homogeneous, and culturally distinct—even with respect to other villages in the commune. Also in physical appearance, the village is compact, clearly bounded, and separated from other villages. One might expect, therefore, that one would at least be able to specify the demographic boundaries of the community at one moment in time.

The simple question of population size, however, became a field problem in determining the operational criteria for "inhabitant." The first task was to determine actual—if not legal— residence. One elderly widow lived in Bruson only during the summer months, spending her winters with a married daughter in another village. I eventually put her name on my list of "inhabitants"—chiefly because I could think of no valid reason to leave her off. By Brusonins she was regarded as a member of the community.

Several young men appeared in the village only on weekends, more or less regularly—working in other Swiss cantons during the week. Since their names appeared on the voter roll of

Bruson, I accepted this as a legal criterion of residence. One of these young men was engaged to a girl from a different canton. I decided that, when he married and established a family of procreation outside the village, I could no longer count him as an "inhabitant" of Bruson—whether or not he remained on the voter roll.

Legal criteria of residence seemed useful operationally—until I realized that one of the official voters in Bruson was an outsider who was leasing a café on the ski slopes. Although he had legal status as a resident of the village, he neither lived within the village boundaries nor was he regarded as a villager by others. When women were enfranchised in 1970 and appeared on the voter roll, I encountered another flaw in my operational device: one of the women on the list was not living in the village—she had been dead for two years.

A man who appeared on the Bruson list of voters—and who was, in fact, one of the village representatives to the commune council—actually lived in another village as a result of his marriage. Born in Bruson, inscribed there officially as a voter, even an important political figure in the village—he could not be put on my list of "inhabitants."

After considerable agonizing, I finally decided to use several—even conflicting—operational criteria in determining the village population. I had become painfully aware of the nature of "reality"—of the elusive correspondence between data and truth.

One clear property of "reality" was its space-time component. The community was certainly homogeneous—and almost entirely endogamous. Knowing that the village had been depopulating since the beginning of the century, I set out to inquire into the nature of this migration. This line of questioning revealed a group of 72 cognates of living resident Brusonins—children and siblings born between 1902 and 1946—who had married out of the village and, as a group, had produced 108 children. Most of these non-resident cognates and their children lived in the canton, if not in the commune itself. Although constituting a spatially dispersed group, these 180 people comprised a second "village of Bruson"—a conceptual "village" of exogamous marriages.

Members of the two "villages," although separated spatially, are in frequent communication with each other. The channels of communication are never closed. In the ordinary case, non-resident cognates will return to Bruson—at least on the occasion of the patron-saint day. Other cases, which seem extraordinary to us, are regarded quite impassively by Bruson-ins: an old spinster who spent forty consecutive years working in Marseilles and returned "home" to retire; a man who went to London at the age of thirty, eventually establishing a hotel there and marrying one of his employees, and returned to the village fifty-five years later; a brother who moved to Canada in the 1920s, leaving inalienable his portion of his father's house; and the man who emigrated to America in 1849, wrote intermit-tently to his cousins in Bagnes, and finally, in 1892, wrote the letter I have already quoted inquiring about his share of his deceased sister's property.

The ties between the two "villages" are very real, even when physical contact between them is infrequent or unlikely. The actual village of Bruson—although small, distinctive, homoge-neous, even endogamous—cannot be understood except as part of this larger entity. The "inhabitants" of Bruson are those who have married endogamously and stayed at home. From this point of view, the "little community" is a spurious commu-nity.

Bruson is not unusual in this regard on the European scene. The *exode rural*, widespread since the beginning of the century and especially fatal in mountain villages, presents the investi-gator with many such spurious communities. Peasant villages which, in the last century, depended on seasonal migration have been depleted through the permanent removal of these mi-grants. The population of the French Alpine commune of St.-Colomban des Villards, for instance, has dropped from 1061 in 1911 to 252 in 1962 (Bozon 1970:271). The commune tradi-tionally supplemented its agro-pastoral subsistence base by sending men into the lowlands—as far off as Grenoble and Marseilles—for winter employment. The traditional occupa-tions were all itinerant: sweeping chimneys, carding flax, and selling dry goods. Men and their sons traced out a sort of human transhumant pattern—coming down from the mountains after the fall harvest, gradually working their way to the cities, and then slowly reascending for spring planting. Modern technology put the chimney sweeps and flax carders out of business—removing an essential portion of their livelihood—and eventually drove them to settle permanently in the cities. The fate of the itinerant merchants was somewhat different, although the outcome for the commune was the same. Those merchants who were able to accumulate sufficient savings invested them in more profitable and reliable shops and became permanent city dwellers.

Where depopulation has been so obvious and drastic, it is not difficult to explain and interpret. In 1907, Bruson—with a population of 500—was described as "the largest village in the Commune, second only to the agglomeration of Le Châble and Villette" (Courthion 1907:133). The comparison of a local census of 1910 with my own in 1969 gave me some clues as to the process of depopulation. There has been a sloughing off of certain families in favor of others—the "core families"—who have direct descendants in the village today. This traceable descent, together with the striking fact of the continuing numerical dominance of these core families, suggests that the demographic depopulation of Bruson has not been accompanied by a social-structural extinction of the village. One can almost say that the Bruson of today is a scaled-down but not significantly altered version of the Bruson of the turn of the century.

In other cases, however, the "little community" one sees today is really deceptive. The French village Roussillon, for instance, has remained apparently stable in the *size*, but not in the *content* of its population. Of the approximately 700 people listed in the censuses of 1946 and 1954, only 275 were the same in both censuses. The other 400 or 500 in each census were all different individuals. Thus, the total number of *different* people living in Roussillon was at least 1150, with only about 700 actually in the commune at the time of each census. The "illusion of demographic stability" depended largely on the existence of the small "core population" of 275 who are property owners and political powers in the commune. In addition, "the people who move into Roussillon are very much like the people who leave ... families of about the same composition and professions" (Wylie 1963:236).

In another Provençal village, Colpied (Reiter 1972), there

has been a replacement of population together with a decline in size. There is a tendency for young people to leave and older people to move in—either city people of retirement age or, more recently, people who commute to jobs outside the commune. Is the "little community" of Colpied the same one which existed during the "Golden Age" of the village, before the "loss of richness" of social relations and institutions? Again one confronts the space-time component of reality, this time in a more subtle sense—for the "Golden Age" of Colpied is variously placed in time by villagers as being "before the War," or "between the two wars." Since the particular dating of the Golden Age seems to correlate with the age of the informant—indeed, seems to refer to his or her youth, a kind of personal Golden Age—the "little community" is fixed in time by subjective measures.

In fact, is not the concept of "little community" wholly subjective—the product of Redfield's admirable but misguided humanism? While it is useful heuristically to measure actual situations against ideal types, one's confidence in such measures might be fortified by some reality in the ideal. If the ideal type does not exist today, in modern Europe, perhaps it did exist sometime in the past—before the post-industrial transformation of traditional peasantries.

I have already noted that, in St.-Colomban des Villards, the traditional economy depended on seasonal migration of certain portions of the population. The same was true in Bruson. Also in other Swiss Alpine villages in the nineteenth century, men engaged in non-agricultural occupations to supplement their work on the land. Törbel, for instance—a village in the German-speaking part of the Valais—was famous for its muleteers, who were put out of business only by the advent of modern transportation methods (Netting 1972). Other villages were known for their artisans, who often travelled part of the year to ply their trade.

Even as early as the ninth century in Frankish Gaul, the feudal domain was populated by a variety of tenants—some permanent and some itinerant. The slave trade, which existed in Roman times and was revived with the Crusades, brought new workers to the feudal community. Some of them worked in slave-gangs, on a temporary and itinerant basis, while others

—called *casati* because they were provided with a house and fields—enjoyed essentially the same status as the free tenants. The ranks of the tenants, both slave and free, were often swelled by temporary agricultural workers—especially at times of peak work such as the harvest. These workers were recruited on the basis of

> seasonal employment, where the demand was for an increased effort over a relatively short period. But the very existence of these temporary workers is an indication of greater mobility among the rural population than is sometimes imagined and also of a margin of surplus labour, attributable no doubt to the low level of cultivation at this period. (Bloch 1966:66-7)

This temporary mobility of the rural population also has taken the form, in various epochs, of religious pilgrimage. In the Middle Ages, for instance, there was a steady traffic across the Great St. Bernard Pass and over the Col de la Fenêtre—then negotiable because of different climatic conditions (Bérard 1963:26ff). Jusserand's delightful book, *English Wayfaring Life in the Middle Ages* (1961), describes the diverse movements of people throughout France and the British Isles, and the hazards attendant upon such travel. Special Swiss versions of temporary migration have taken rural people into cities to work in the hotel industry, and into foreign countries to serve as mercenary soldiers. In both circumstances, the returning individuals were agents of change.

A folk tale of Bagnes has as its protagonist—and ultimately, its true hero—

> an aging veteran of Marignano [the 1515 battle in which the Swiss were defeated by the French] ... recently returned from France with an entire repertoire of novelties, tricks, and the vocabulary of the military camp; this was Thémistocle Guigoz of Montagnier, the first to bring tobacco to the tight-fisted [people of Bagnes]. (Courthion 1893:281)

According to the legend, the parish priest was in league with the people of Val d'Aosta—traditional ememies of Bagnes—and had promised to deliver the entire Bagnard population to the Valdôtains. His device was to urge all people to attend church on the appointed Sunday when he would deliver a "long and very important sermon." On the fateful day, only the old mercenary failed to attend church. "He was walking around his room smoking"—and, presumably, also swearing, true to the nature of a confirmed sinner—when he spotted the Valdô-tain armies coming over the pass into the valley of Bagnes. He put on his suit of armor and helmet, mounted his white horse—white, of course, because he was about to become a hero—and rushed to the church to expose the treacherous priest. Then he led the men of Bagnes—"armed with scythes, pitch-forks, axes, and cudgels" (the traditional weaponry of peasant armies)—to a crushing victory over the invaders.

The mercenary Guigoz, in spite of—or, rather, because of—his sinful ways acquired abroad, brought a bit of pleasure to his stay-at-home fellows in the form of tobacco, and ultimately was their savior—the anti-hero who exposes the perfidy of God's representative on earth.

While this story is legendary, there is a historical episode in the life of Bagnes which provides another example of the prevalence and influence of migration. In this case, the migrant —although a Valaisan—was a stranger to the commune. Maurice Farinet (Ramuz 1968), apprenticed in the 1860s to an old man, inherited from him the secret of a gold lode in the mountains. Farinet took up the occupation of making counterfeit money, which he freely distributed among his friends. Hunted con-stantly by the police, he was regarded as a champion of the little people by his fellows, who claimed that Farinet's coins were "better"—that is, contained more gold—than those of the government. Being independently wealthy, so to speak, he lived a life of leisure—never forgetting, though, his debt to and love for the mountains. He is described as having brought poetry, music, dancing, and gaiety to the people of Bagnes, among whom he lived for a time. The grateful people, especially his Bagnard mistress, did all they could to hide him from the authorities, but he was finally "hunted down like an animal."

Guigoz and Farinet—both actors in the larger political arena —are particularly fitting expressions of Bagnard tradition: the skeptical attitude toward the Church, the militant readiness to defend the territory, the "progressive" acceptance of new goods and ideas, and the ultimate scorn for outside authority—

whether eccleciastical or temporal. All these aspects of Bagnard culture attest to the fact of long-standing openness of the society. The mercenary and the counterfeiter have survived in legend and history only because they were especially colorful figures. My historical and ethnographic survey, however, amply demonstrates that they were not unique. Peasants move in and out of "little communities" freely and widely—for economic or religious or political reasons, on a seasonal or longer-term basis.

Within the community itself, one can often read the dialogue between Great and Little Traditions, an exchange which has left behind institutions or their evolutionary transformations. One such study unfolds the adaptive transformations of *compadrazgo*—ritual godparenthood—in Europe and Latin America (Mintz and Wolf 1950). This Roman Catholic institution—the ceremonial sponsorship of an individual in major life-crisis rites—creates ties of ritual kinship between the actual parents and the godparents of the individual. Because compadrazgo involves the co-parents in all the obligations, prescriptions, and privileges of actual kinship, it extends the kin network, thus increasing the scope of obligatory mutual-aid relationships. Used vertically—by enlisting godparents of higher social status and power—it is a characteristic feature of patronage systems.

Mintz and Wolf document the peasants' manipulation of compadrazgo as a regulatory mechanism responding to the pressures of a particular time. In the twelfth and thirteenth centuries, for example, the peasants' struggle for release from the oppressive bonds of feudalism was aided by their increasing emphasis on horizontal compadrazgo—"to solidify social relationships horizontally among members of the same rural neighborhood" (Mintz and Wolf 1950:181). Compadrazgo was an adaptive mechanism which enabled the peasant to defend himself—originally, by cementing good relations with his feudal lord and, later, by freeing himself from noble bondage.

Another example of the response of the peasantry to threatening forces from its environment is the device of community closure. Far from being evidence in support of Redfield's ideal "little community"—which is implicitly closed—the Mesoamerican "closed corporate community" described by Wolf (1957) represents an adaptive strategy. Although community closure was initiated by the Spanish *conquistadores*, it has been maintained by villagers as a defensive mechanism in the "dualization of society into a dominant entrepreneurial sector and a dominated sector of native peasants" (Wolf 1957:237). The closed corporate community, with its strong ethos of egalitarianism implemented by various devices to level wealth differentials, is a bastion of security for its members who, while sharing their poverty, also share in and thereby diminish their life risks.

Many mechanisms seen in ethnographic studies attest to the reality of relations between the "little community" and its environment. I have indicated the difficulty of determining meaningful cultural boundaries of the peasant community. Where boundaries could be determined, they were regularly blurred by a flow of people and ideas. In many instances, the peasantry manipulated elements from the Great Tradition. And, in the limiting case, community closure itself became an adaptive mechanism for dealing with outside pressures, demonstrating that the peasantry has always been an open, dynamic socio-cultural system.

18. The Part-Society Concept

Another implication of the "little community" concept is an image of the peasantry as one among several unlike components of a larger system. Cultural distinctiveness was the basis of Kroeber's characterization of the peasantry as a part-society with a part-culture. Redfield's "little community" extended the image, almost to the point of describing the peasantry as a "society apart." But other components of the larger system also display cultural distinctiveness without being closed part-societies.

In feudal Europe, the system which embraced all these distinctive but interacting components—nobility, church, *bourgeoisie*, peasantry—is an example of what we call the state. Wolf argues convincingly that the state may take various forms and its seat of power may be variously located—as long as it represents "the crystallization of executive power":

> Not the city, but the state is the decisive criterion of civilization and it is the appearance of the state which marks the threshold of transition between food cultivators in general and peasants. Thus, it is only when a cultivator is integrated into a society with a state—that is, when the cultivator becomes subject to the demands and sanctions of power-holders outside his social stratum—that we can appropriately speak of peasantry. (Wolf 1966b:11)

Wolf's state reminds one of Redfield's civilization. It is not so much a specific political or administrative structure as a system of relationships. It consists of social strata with differential power over one another. Integration of these strata is founded on the common recognition of an overriding executive power. But integration is also based on interdependence. To view the system as an ordered hierarchy of increasing power over and subjugation of the next lower level is to lose a great deal of information and insight. Such a view leads to a higher abstraction of the system, still further from reality, as binary, unidirectional, and ultimately, exploitative: the state vs. the peasantry, with the state always winning.

Ethnographic and historical data suggest a very different kind of relationship between the peasant and the "power-holders outside his social stratum." In medieval Europe, these power-holders might belong to one of several social strata. Furthermore, their "demands and sanctions" might be aimed only incidentally at the peasant as part of their own power struggles with other components of the system. Finally, the peasant not only reacted but also responded to these demands —for example, by allying himself temporarily with one or another group.

Nowhere does Wolf say or imply that the demands themselves must be exploitative. Indeed, the classic feudal structure was based on an expectation of mutual rewards—protection from the lord, produce and labor from the peasant. When this expectation was not satisfied, each side had its unique arsenal of weapons. A typical peasant weapon was concealing information about crop yield. Beginning in the seventeenth century, the lord might counter by hiring "commissioners" to search through old records to create—or fabricate—a land cadaster which enormously increased the lord's revenue and his control over his peasants (Bloch 1966:130ff). If, however, the lord's demands became too great and the rewards too small, the peasants readily took to their pitchforks and axes; but the essence of the system, for each side, was to preserve the other in reasonably operative condition.

In feudal Europe, the system of relationships which Wolf envisages as the "state" was expressed as several culturally distinct social sectors. The sector of peasant cultivators was "subject to the demands and sanctions of power-holders" in other sectors. Although numerically superior, the peasantry had little direct access to political or economic control and so was dominated by other sectors. Yet domination could never be allowed to proceed to the point of destruction, since the other "parts" of the whole society depended on the peasantry for food and labor. The local community—a seigneurial domain —was economically diversified and largely self-sufficient. It was not, however, politically or socially autonomous, because the seigneur himself was "subject to the demands and sanctions of powerholders outside his social stratum."

Our image of the feudal state seems to be a realization of the modern policy-maker's dream: a solidary and dependable economic and social base at the local level, regulated politically from above. This is, at least, the dream of the highly centralized European states like France. With the loss of definition of social sectors—through bureaucratization of the state and capitalization of the entire economy—the modern state pursues more or less consistent and effective policies to maintain the peasant sector. It offers direct subsidies to small-scale agriculture and indirect subsidies in the form of social welfare support for the aged, grants to permit the education of children, retirement pensions. Simultaneously, the state attempts to capitalize peasant farming by encouraging "rationalization" of farming and by offering subsidies to create "more productive" systems of monoculture.

Sometimes—as in the case of the Alpine regions—the conversion is from polycultural "unproductive" farming to a kind of "monoculture" based on tourism or industry. The stated objectives of all these efforts are to maintain some portion of the population in agriculture—at least on a part-time basis—and to reverse the *exode rural* which began with the eighteenth-century Agricultural Revolution (Bloch 1966:230ff) and which has grown with increasing intensity to the present day. Witness the following statement, from a Swiss publication based on official government sources:

> One of the main aims of Swiss agrarian policy is to maintain an efficient farming community that can be relied upon in the event of food imports being restricted or cut off. Despite profound

changes in agriculture and its role within the economic framework during the past decades, Switzerland can still produce as great a part of its food as hitherto.... Though the population keeps growing and the area under cultivation diminishes constantly, today, as twenty years ago, our agriculture provides between 55% and 60% of our food needs, depending on the harvest. During the Second World War it climbed to about 70%.... In the alpine regions, where the problems are rather different, efforts to foster the tourist industry and create new jobs through other branches of the economy have helped to preserve the farming community and stem the flood of population away from the alpine valleys. (Kümmerly and Frey 1962:41)

The implicit goals, however, are to integrate the peasantry into the capitalist system of production—that is, to make the peasantry a more "organic" part of the larger society. The peasantry was an integral part of the fabric of pre-industrial society—one of several distinct but interacting sectors. In modern Europe, however, the peasantry is not "organic"—neither in the sense of distinctive nor in the sense of vital. The complexity of the modern state is not founded on the coordination of diverse and essential parts but has been concentrated in the sphere of industrial capitalism and in the hands of businessmen and bureaucrats. What has been lost is the distinctiveness of the constituent "parts" of the "whole" and their consequent richness of interdependence. The components of the new social order now owe their survival to their standardized binary relations with the faceless state. Agriculture, for example, is equated with and reduced to a form of industrial capitalism—another "production" element contributing to the gross national product and regulated by the needs of the political economy of the state.

In feudal Europe, the whole consisted of several distinct parts, integrated partly by the activities of a centralized executive. Each part made its unique contribution to the economic or social fabric of the whole, and each was subject to "demands and sanctions"—political or economic—from each of the others. Feudal Europe, then, was a combinatorial system of functional interdependencies—in Wolf's terms, a set of power relationships whose content might be political or economic. Based on clearly delineated components, feudal society's complexity lay in the richness and strength of connections. In such a system, there could be no simple, permanent, binary relationship. Even unmistakable exploitation is better understood as a limiting case of functional dependence—"dependence" in the simple mathematical sense—of parts of the system.

But in modern European society, the vastness and diversity are supported by internal simplification—reduction in the kinds of components and bureaucratic homogenization of connections. Although several "parts" still remain in the modern system, they are so vitiated by the loss of variety as to have no relation whatever to each other except as equal members of the whole. In the extreme case of state centralization, such as in France, one may imagine the kind of "tree" which mathematicians describe as multi-leveled (highly intermediated) and low in branching (having a small span of control). Each level of the tree represents a level of the political-administrative bureaucracy, beginning with the central government in Paris, moving down through various regional subdivisions, and ending in the commune.

This structure was created by the Constituent Assembly in 1789 and has remained essentially the same to the present day. Although the original objective was to decentralize the government out of respect for the variety of local concerns, the standardized structure allowed for no modification in case of a change in local conditions. The structure hardened into a rigid top-heavy hierarchy which spread to non-administrative domains of activity. This was a case of atomization of control with only a mechanical and vertical coordination of parts. Each new pair of related branches was quickly "coiffed" by a third, higher-level, controlling node. Local affairs came to be more and more dominated by the concerns of the state.

The span of control—and the span of vision—is unitary in this tree: each node is in direct contact only with its immediate superior and inferior. From the point of view of any particular social sector at the bottom—the peasantry, for instance—all the nodes and branches above it in the political hierarchy might just as well be collapsed into a single level with a single superior node: "the state." Any intermediate levels are simply representatives of the state, and, for this reason, they serve only to replicate the same bureaucratic process.

From an evolutionary perspective, the atomization and homogenization of "part-societies" reduced the diversity of connections among them, as each came to interact more and more exclusively with the central bureaucracy. As a result, the integration of the "whole"—the state—was transformed from a truly organic to a simple hierarchic system—an impersonal undifferentiated organization in which each part was in direct contact only with the central bureaucracy and, thus, could change or be changed with minimal disturbance to the others. The modern centralized state, having taken unto itself the functions of subjection and protection, is now the chief "power-holder" pressing "demands and sanctions" down to the various social sectors, peasantry included.

19. Cultural Pluralism and Political Federalism

Because the centralized nation-state is the most typical form of modern political organization, there are compelling reasons to study the anomalous case of Switzerland. This modern, industrial, capitalist, democratic state in the very center of Western Europe has a long history of cultural deviance within the European community. The Swiss version of federalism is the antithesis of the centralized, hierarchic model of the state. Although at first glance one sees a state comparable to other European states, one soon discovers anomaly and paradox. For example, the Canton of Valais has more banks per capita than any other Swiss canton. Knowing that the Valais is an agricultural mountain canton, one might interpret this fact to mean that the proverbial Swiss bankers have found perfect victims and are exploiting this more conservative and less sophisticated segment of the population. On closer examination, however, one discovers that this impressive number of banks includes a large number of locally-controlled, cooperative savings and loan associations (the Raiffeisen banks) as well as small, privately-owned banks existing in only one community and not associated with any of the large, nationwide banking corporations. Other examples would similarly reveal the peculiar combination of egalitarian individualism, of communitarian capitalism, that are basic to Swiss culture.

These apparent paradoxes—the modern transformations of Alpine political and social ideologies which created a chain of autonomous "republics" in the Middle Ages—are supported structurally by the modern federalist system and are being threatened increasingly as the Swiss state is drawn more and more into the international system. By studying Swiss political organization, then, we are studying an acephalous, nonhierarchic state with a high degree of cultural continuity which is now struggling to maintain its identity in a rapidly changing environment. Swiss federalist ideology—a political abstraction from enormous cultural, ecological, and historical diversity—is, more than an ideology, an organizational principle and a frame of reference in which political behavior is played out. Indeed, it is a special articulation of the part-whole relationship, a viable alternative to the crushing hierarchic weight of the centralized state.

In the three-tiered Swiss political system—confederation, canton, and commune—the commune has temporal primacy. The 1291 Pact of the Forest States, which created the nucleus of the modern Confederation, was an agreement among autonomous local communities to surrender some of their sovereignty for purposes of defense and survival. The Pact formed a loose, essentially military alliance among the member communities. It stated:

> In view of the troubled times, the men of the Valley of Uri, the moot of the Valley of Schwyz and the community of the Lower Valley of Unterwalden have, for the better protection and seemly preservation of them and theirs, most faithfully vowed: to stand by one another with help, advice and all favor, with their lives and worldly goods, within and without the Valleys, with might and main against all and every man that dare do them all, or any one of them, ill, either by force, annoyance or injury done or intended to their life and goods. (Kümmerly and Frey 1962)

As additional members joined the Confederation—eventually larger agglomerations called "cantons"—a second and complementary objective was added to the original one of preserving the autonomy of member "states": to guarantee the free movement and residence of their citizens throughout the Confederation. This new political status of *confédéré* (citizen of the Confederation), formalized in the 1848 Constitution, was inspired by the French Revolutionary ideals of equality and fraternity. The cultural heterogeneity of the Swiss state made such personal guarantees essential, far beyond the dictates of humanism. Ultimately, these constitutional guarantees provided the necessary scale for a modern economy. Both principles of Confederation—the autonomy of member "states" and the rights of confédérés—are embodied in the modern bicameral legislature: the Conseil National represents the people directly, its deputies elected by a system of proportional representation; the Conseil des Etats gives equal representation to each sovereign "state" within the Confederation, its members elected by a method agreed upon locally in each canton.

The modern commune jealously guards its position as the keystone of the political structure. Politically and economically, it remains to a large extent the primary unit in the system. It has, for example, first authority over citizenship: every Swiss citizen, whether native or naturalized, must be accepted as a member of this fundamental community. Once a member, he and his male descendants remain members essentially forever, regardless of their actual residence. The Commune of Bagnes, thus, officially consists of 11,000 *bourgeois* (commune citizens)—only 4,800 of whom presently live on commune territory.

The bourgeois of a commune form a corporate territorial unit with a unique history founded on tradition, custom, and genealogical continuity. The contemporary witness to this history is the "patrimony" of the commune—the ownership and management of its inviolate territory. Although only the bourgeois actually own and manage the territory, all legal residents in the commune have use rights—at the pleasure and under the control of the bourgeois. The commune has its own financial resources—collecting revenues from its property, taxing all residents for specific services provided, and levying taxes in the form of cash payments or labor corvées.

The commune legislates and executes its own affairs. Ultimate legislative power rests in the hands of the residents who, in the larger communes, are represented by an elected council— called, in the Valais, the *conseil général*. This legislative council must, for example, approve the budget and the accounts presented to it by the executive body—called the *conseil communal* in the Valais. In case of nonapproval, the canton intervenes as arbiter. Similarly, while the commune employs its own police force and elects its own magistrates to deal with minor breaches of civil law, the canton is responsible for major civil and criminal litigation and also provides courts of appeal. The essence of these cantonal functions, however, is the preservation of communal autonomy (in the realm of finance) and the protection of individual civil liberties (in the realm of justice) according to guidelines set by the federal constitution. In short, then, the commune, as a political and economic corporation,

> has the right to administer itself freely, within the limits set by the Constitution and the law, or, often, by local traditions and precedents of jurisprudence.... The commune provides, on a small scale, approximately the same public services as the state. Ordinarily, it has police to assure its territorial security; frequently, too, it organizes religious practice and public instruction; it maintains or subsidizes museums, libraries, theaters; through its rural employees, it surveys the maintenance of its land; it maintains public buildings, roads, lighting, fire prevention; in most cantons, the commune assists the indigent and ill; one of its principal prerogatives is the right to manage its own patrimony. (Sauser-Hall 1965:177-178)

Within each canton, there is enormous diversity in the number, size, composition, and organization of its communes. In addition to the political commune described above, there may be other cross-cutting units: the *commune bourgeoise*, consisting only of actual citizens; the *commune scolaire*, specifically charged with public instruction; the *commune ecclésiastique*—essentially, the parish; the *commune d'assistance*, consisting of those citizens who have the right to public

assistance. The political communes may range in size from 80
people living in a single village to 4,000 or more—as in the case
of Bagnes—occupying several villages and hamlets.

The political and the bourgeoise communes may coincide
in their membership or they may be widely separated. In the
Valaisan commune of Zermatt, for instance, only 200 of the
700 resident households are bourgeois and, therefore, exclusive
owners of the territory which has become so valuable with the
development of tourism. The commune may be primarily agricultural, touristic, or industrial. It may by urban or rural,
and—within the rural category—a mountain or a lowland commune. The mountain commune of Bagnes, for instance, is
economically a mixture of agriculture, tourism, and tourism-
related industry.

Politically, the commune may be, by tradition, conservative,
radical, or mixed. Some communes—especially in the Lower
Valais—are famous for their support of the anticlerical movement in the mid-nineteenth century and for their receptiveness
to church reformation even earlier. Others are known for their
maintenance of family politics and their resistance to allying
themselves with cantonally-organized political parties. Still
others are noticed because of a sudden wholesale switch in
support from one major party to the other. Some communes
threw off the yoke of feudal allegiance before the fourteenth
century, while others remained subjects until the French Revolution. In Bagnes—as in other mountain communes—feudalism
was weakly expressed. For the past century, the commune of
Bagnes has been politically conservative but is also known for
its history of anticlericalism and radicalism—both of which
survive on the political scene in the form of a minority party.

There are also wide differences among communes with respect to their relative participation in the capital-
ist-bureaucratic system of the state. Some communes of peasant farming where the land allows a high degree of
mechanization have been readily transformed into large-scale
industrial farming areas. At the other extreme, some mountain
communes of marginal agriculture and no possibilities for
tourism have become bedroom suburbs for nearby industrial
cities.

Swiss federalism originated in and rests upon the combination of commune autonomy and the wide range of diversity among communes. The political power of the commune—its capacity for action—is restrained only insofar as an action might endanger either the existence of the commune or the constitutional liberties of its citizens. Restraint is usually applied by the canton—one of the member "states" in the Confederation with whom it shares sovereignty.

The political and ideological environment of the commune is well expressed in the following discussion by an eminent Swiss jurist on the difference he draws between a "nation" and a "state." Whereas a "nation" may be formed of a population homogeneous in "race, language, religion, customs or political tradition,"

> none of these elements is sufficient by itself to make a nation. What is necessary above all is that the participating peoples have *the desire to be unified*, that they have the same hopes, the same memories, that their history has actually created a *common soul*. The nation is not, therefore, necessarily identical with the State; there are States formed of several nations: the most striking example for a long time was Austria-Hungary which counted among its citizens Germans, Magyars, Italians, Roumanians, and Slavs of various races—Poles, Czechs, Serbs, etc.; they formed a State, they did not constitute a nation. But there are also States consisting only of people having the same *national sentiment*: these are France, Italy, Belgium—although inhabited by Walloons and Flemish—and also Switzerland which—by bringing together three peoples of different race, language, and religion, but inspired by the same political ideal, the same sentiments of independence, and the same traditional will to remain unified —has truly given the nation its highest meaning: a voluntary grouping of populations with common aspirations. (Sauser-Hall 1965:18-19)

The author points out that a "state"—but not a "nation"—may be divided and destroyed by a multiplicity of ethnic, linguistic, and religious groups within its boundaries. He suggests the following tests for true "nationhood":

> We must look into the history, seek out above all the wishes of the population, examine their sentiments for independence, uncover their desire to escape the oppressive power of a State.

The belief of a people—even a composite people—in its political
unity, and its desire to live as a collectivity, are the best
foundations for a nation. (Sauser-Hall 1965:19-20)

Sauser-Hall's distinction between "nation" and "state" high-
lights the unique Swiss formula for political organization: the
dialectic between "independence" and "collectivity." Even his
double reference to "state" is peculiarly Swiss: the "oppressive
power" of the state may emanate from without—from a foreign
state—or from within—from one's own political bureaucracy.
Nor is it surprising to learn that the Swiss were inspired by
American constitutionalists in framing their own modern constitution of 1848. One recalls, for instance, Jefferson's admoni-
tion: "The price of liberty is eternal vigilance."

But, in spite of a discomforting twinge of romanticism in
this Swiss view of the state, one is impressed by the confronta-
tion of a fundamental problem: how to organize cultural
pluralism, how to exploit it to create a unified "nation," how
to prevent its degeneration into the kind of weak segmented
society described by Moore:

Indian society, as many scholars have remarked, resembles some
huge yet very simple invertebrate organism. . . . Through much
of Indian history down to modern times, there was no central
authority imposing its will on the whole subcontinent. Indian
society reminds one of the starfish whom fishermen used to shred
angrily into bits, after which each fragment would grow into
a new starfish. But the analogy is inexact. Indian society was
even simpler and yet more differentiated. Climate, agricultural
practices, taxation systems, religious beliefs, and many other
social and cultural features differed markedly from one part of
the country to another. Caste, on the other hand, was common
to them all and provided the framework around which all of
life was everywhere organized. It made possible these differences
and a society where a territorial segment could be cut off from
the rest without damage, or at least without fatal damage, to
itself or the rest of society. Far more important . . . is the reverse
of this feature. Any attempt at innovation, any local variation,
simply became the basis of another caste. (Moore 1967:458)

The Swiss Confederation, on the other hand, might be described as a simple *vertebrate* organism. It was formed by a

process of accretion over a period of 500 years. Each new member was permitted to retain its own political and cultural forms as long as it submitted to the basic principles of respecting and defending the autonomy of other members and of permitting within its borders the free passage and residence of confédérés—citizens of other cantons. The cantons, thus, are the vertebrae of the organism, and the federalist principles the connective tissue—both together providing internal and external structure and strength. The analogy is even more striking when one recalls that vertebrate organisms are distinguished from lower forms by their relative decentralization of control.

Administrative modernization and consolidation grew gradually. The administrative state was codified in the Constitution of 1848 which also expanded the political ideology to prescribe specifically democratic forms of government for all the cantons. Beyond that prescription, cantonal autonomy continued to be respected and supported. In India, a rigid hierarchy of political and social inequality—the caste system—was the common unifying feature in the enormous regional diversity. The Swiss state, however, rests on an egalitarian political ideology, an efficient and unobtrusive federal administration, diffuseness of political control, and concentration of executive power at the lowest possible level.

The problem of organizing cultural pluralism at the federal level is solved by inverting the normal chain of command and maintaining control at the lowest level: the culturally homogeneous commune. At this level, both opposition and innovation are handled in essentially face-to-face relations among equals. Local autonomy makes possible regional and national diversity.

Even within the commune—especially a large commune like Bagnes—there is a sense of the interplay between uniformity and diversity. Residents of Bruson refer to their canton as *"l'Etat"* and their commune as *"notre république bagnarde."* Within the commune, however, they perceive regional differences based on geography, economy, language, political party affiliation, and a generalized category of *"mentalité."* The different "regions" have different interests and problems. These are represented in the conseil communal—the executive body of commune government. Significantly, it is only at the commune level that initiative and referendum do not exist—on the assumption that this is the level of "pure" democracy, of the direct expression and implementation of the people's wishes. At this level, consensus is the preferred method of decision making, and proportional representation, the instituted method of electing officials.

In this acephalous state with a high degree of distinctiveness of parts based on local power and autonomy, how can one describe the set of relationships, the product of the connections among parts, that is the "state"? Is the part-society concept, as expressed in the following statement, a useful heuristic for understanding the Swiss system?

> What goes on in Gopalpur, India, or Alcalá de la Sierra in Spain cannot be explained in terms of that village alone; the explanation must include consideration both of the outside forces impinging on these villages and of the reactions of villagers to these forces. (Wolf 1966b:1)

In spite of the Swiss inversion of the control hierarchy and the emphasis on local autonomy, the resulting distinctiveness of parts—whether political communes or ecological regions or social sectors—does indeed present a picture of "outside forces impinging on" the village.

To paraphrase Wolf, "what goes on in Bruson cannot be explained in terms of that village alone." What goes on in Bruson is, for instance, a function of what goes on in Verbier, another village in the commune: the peculiar combination of events in that international tourist resort that are "good for" Bruson—tourist revenues for the commune coffers, and the overflow of skiers who find their way to the smaller development in Bruson—and "bad for" Bruson—the enormous land specu-lation by outsiders that makes Brusonins wary of their own developing resort, and the danger to small shops represented by the advent of a national chain-supermarket in Verbier.

The Verbier boom has also given a boost to local industries such as construction and hotels and, thus, has provided in-creased employment opportunities within the commune. But in this context one must also know something of what goes on in Bern, the federal capital. In 1972, as a consequence of the international monetary crisis, the federal government put a temporary ban on sales of land or real estate to non-Swiss. Though clearly a "good thing" for the nation as a whole, the ban is a "bad thing" for the promoters, real estate agents, builders, and construction workers—both in Verbier and in the commune as a whole.

An additional source of revenue for the commune, shared by all the villages, is the hydroelectric plant at the end of the valley. Since the plant and its water sources are on commune territory, all its customers pay the commune. During the immediate postwar years, the construction of the dam provided employment for local men; now the dam has become a tourist attraction, revitalizing the economy of the Upper Valley of Bagnes.

What goes on in Bruson is also a function of what goes on in several neighboring communes where small factories have been established with the help of federal and cantonal subsidies —providing an economic alternative to full-time agriculture. The watch factory in Vollèges has been employing women of Bagnes for several years now, and the more recent electrical applicance factory in Sembrancher will undoubtedly attract both men and women from Bagnes—as a similar factory has done in the mountain commune of Hérémence. At the same time, however, Bruson is one of several sites where federal experimental agricultural stations have been created in the commune—for the expressed purpose of improving the technology of mountain agriculture and dairying.

What goes on in Bruson is also a function of what goes on in Sion, the cantonal capital. The canton controls prices of staples like bread and dairy products. It encourages the formation of agricultural cooperatives—offering subsidies and experts for technological improvement, and chartering these cooperatives to maintain quality control. In the 1930s, when the canton drained the marshland of the Rhône Valley to create enormously productive garden land, what happened in Sion was the beginning of a schism between mountain and lowland agriculturalists. But, for a long time before that, what had been going on in the Rhône Valley had had its effects on Bruson. In the nineteenth century, the Rhône Valley was a market for the surplus crops of Bruson: apples, cherries, and pears were sold to the preserve factory in Saxon; honey, cheese, and grain to the people of Fully and other communes.

The distinctiveness of parts in the Swiss system and their functional interdependence are implicit in all these economic relations. The Brusonin is consumer of manufactured products; rural producer supplying food to the urban sector and raw materials to agricultural processing industries; mountain agriculturalist in competition with lowland farmers for economic and political support; owner and manager of recreational property for city dwellers; part-time laborer or craftsman supplying goods and services to tourists. Or one may choose "parts" in other ways. The Brusonin belongs to the "state religion" of his canton; he is in the linguistic majority in his bilingual canton but minority in the Confederation; he is a bourgeois of his commune and so participates in the political, social, and economic benefits that derive from the commune's autonomy in the larger political structure.

These data do indeed reveal that Bruson is a part-society which can be understood only by considering the "outside forces impinging on" the village—whether those forces emanate from other villages in the commune, from other communes, from the cantonal or the federal level. How, then, can one argue that the Swiss political system is qualitiatively different from that of a centralized hierarchic state? The difference lies in the *response* to these outside forces—a response predicated on the universal Swiss fear of growing centralization. To the extent that the Swiss political system is qualitatively different from international "whole," some unilateral federal decisions do penetrate the ideological fabric—for example, the federal regulation of land sales in 1972. In other cases, however—especially in domestic affairs—federalist ideology prevents or moderates such unilateral action. The recent controversy over land-use planning is an instructive example of dialogue and negotiation between various levels in the political structure.

In 1969 the Swiss people overwhelmingly voted for a constitutional amendment for the protection of the natural environment. Since the laws necessary for implementation of this amendment would not be ready for a popular vote until 1974, the federal government proposed a provisional ordinance to set aside certain lands as "green zones," forbidden to construction. Under certain conditions, however, a canton could make exceptions in particular cases. The people accepted this ordinance in 1971, and the government then presented its provisional plan to the cantons for approval or amendment. At that time, the government of the Canton of Valais objected to the magnitude of green zones proposed by the Confederation and created its own special commission to study the matter locally and propose an alternative plan. The commission, acting in the name of the cantonal executive branch, requested that each commune submit a zoning plan for its own territory. Since very few communes responded, the commission drew up a comprehensive plan for the canton as a whole and submitted the appropriate portions to each commune for study.

Any individual landowner had the right to appeal the zoning proposed for his lands, and the official appeal form was published in the daily newspaper. Over 14,000 appeals were received by the Valaisan government and many tens of thousands by cantonal governments throughout the country. The extent of opposition at the level of the citizenry transformed individual objections into a potential mass political response.

Opposition at the commune level, too, was expressed in political terms. Valaisan communes received the canton's zoning plan as a political affront, an infringement on their autonomy. It became clear that many of the communes that had not responded to the Canton's original request had been acting in defiance. Those few that had responded now claimed that their zoning plans had not been considered by the special commission. At bottom, of course, was the sudden realization on the part of individual citizens that the costs of enacting the ideal of environmental protection were to be their own out-of-pocket costs. Long-term plans to build a house for one's married son on land acquired gradually over the years, and short-term plans to build tourist chalets for income—these could be wiped out by the stroke of a drafting pen on a map, a stroke probably made by some urban planner who understood nothing of rural society.

The matter was aired in the cantonal legislature—the Grand Conseil, whose members are elected as representatives from local districts. The legislators raised serious and indignant questions about the actual powers of the canton government vis-à-vis both the Confederation and the communes, suggesting

that the canton had not provided aggressive leadership at the
federal level. They also demanded to know the names of the
members of the special commission, suggesting that these
people were not truly representative of local commune interests. Finally, a large majority of the legislators openly re-
nounced their own party colleagues in the executive branch,
the Conseil d'Etat, and passed a motion to revoke the plan
of the special commission on zoning.

The case is still pending resolution, but even at this point
one can see certain important principles at work: formal and
informal defiance of higher authority, conciliatory action on
the part of these authorities, the unity and solidarity of the
canton in the face of encroaching centralization of power, and
the intra-cantonal "federalism" expressed by the communes.
The defense of federalism was put in modern terms by the
Socialist press of the Valais: "The worst enemies of federalism
are those who by their immobility and their 'cantonism,'
provoke the intervention of Bern. If we are not willing to put
our own house in order, then others will do it for us, and in
a manner that does not suit us" (Rosset 1973). Considering
that the Socialists are the only major party favoring federal
centralization, one is all the more struck by this defense of
federalist principles. The argument against "immobility" and
"cantonism" is a plea to set aside a reactionary provincialism
in favor of a more dynamic and offensive stance: in short, equal
participation in the game of decision making.

Although there are indeed "outside forces impinging" on
successively lower levels in the political structure, Swiss federalism—both as a legal and an ideological system—excludes the
status of *absolute* power-holder. As one ascends in the structure, one finds fewer politicians and more administrators. The
federal executive itself is a group of seven men drawn from
various non-political professions who rotate annually to serve
as President of the Confederation.

Far from being an undifferentiated, top-heavy bureaucracy,
the Swiss state is a complex and multifaceted set of shifting
relationships—the most important of which are the closest. The
village operates in the political environment of a national
ideology of federalism, the idea of a voluntary grouping of
autonomous units living in a collectivity. The political under-

pinnings of this collectivity are the diffuseness of executive control and the concentration of each type of power at the lowest possible level of the hierarchy. Cultural pluralism is sustained by political pluralism. The organic integration of this acephalous state is based on a historical tradition of federal heterogeneity and local homogeneity.

I showed how the Swiss Confederation grew from a military alliance among distinctive and autonomous political entities. These entities were not "power-holders" in any sense but rather agro-pastoral mountain communities unified internally by their economic activities and kinship ties. The Forest States which made the original covenant of confederation probably conceived of themselves primarily as economic corporations (*Allmeinden*) —exploiting a certain territory and marketing their surpluses in a central market. Political awareness probably came later, and the members of the Allmeinde became citizens participating in the political *Landsgemeinde*.

The Valaisan version of this history, although not well documented, was probably very similar. One of the oldest surviving institutions specific to Valaisan society is the *consortage*. In the Commune of Bagnes, the consortages existed at least as early as 1625, at which time the political commune entered into formal written agreement with the cooperatives of each village to create a more equitable distribution of use-rights in the bourgeois-owned summer pasturelands (Courthion 1907:266). The system of irrigation canals (*bisses*) is at least two centuries older (Bérard 1963:25). Economic historians hypothesize that these local economic associations predated the commune as a political entity (Bergier 1968:37).

The early Confederation, then, was composed of autonomous, economically integrated communities allied to preserve their autonomy and their distinctiveness. Napoleon imposed a French-style bureaucratic structure on this loose alliance— creating a "Helvetian Republic." The administrative hierarchy survived his defeat but became a Swiss-style bureaucratic structure with its major function the continued preservation of local autonomy.

20. The Nested Political System

The highly centralized and intermediated heirarchy that is the modern French state is a classic example of what Bailey has called "encapsulation" (1969:146ff). Encapsulation is a political phenomenon which penetrates the economic and social life of the community. In Wissous, for example (R. T. and G. Anderson 1962), the larger political structure was imitated in the bureaucratization of voluntary associations. What happens in Wissous cannot be understood without knowing what is happening in Paris. In Wissous the "peasant dilemma" (Wolf 1966b:12ff) has been resolved in favor of the non-peasant sector of the social order. Where there is no longer a peasantry, there can hardly be a peasant dilemma.

The Wissous "solution" is characteristically French. In fact, any form of encapsulation—incorporation into the larger state structure—would be predictable in France. The Provençal village of Colpied, for instance, has been encapsulated through monoculturization of its agriculture and the transfer of control to higher levels in the hierarchy (Reiter 1972). The Alpine village of St.-Véran (Burns 1959) has been encapsulated through transformation into a community of "park-keeper peasants" (Franklin 1969:220ff).

In all these cases of encapsulation, one common feature emerges: the simplification of the traditional community structure—economic, social, and political—so it may slide easily into a slot in the national hierarchy. The community's loss is the state's gain. The community contributes to the welfare of the state by reducing its internal variation to an absolute minimum. The process, of course, also reduces the adaptability of the community and renders it a dependent cog in the state machinery: the heavily intermediated hierarchy collapses into a simple two-level hierarchy. The peasant dilemma of choosing between unsatisfactory alternatives is now reduced to one of maintaining a position at the lower level, of keeping up with the "demands and sanctions" set by the higher level. There are no longer countervailing and sometimes contradictory internal requirements. Wissous is, simply, a Parisian suburb, Colpied a lavender-growing village, St.-Véran a ski resort.

In the Swiss state, however—with its inverted political hierarchy—local diversity is not only preserved but also encouraged. The case of the Valaisan commune of Hérémence is instructive. Although traditionally an agro-pastoral commune, the terrain and steep slope of commune land made agriculture less profitable and less appealing as industry appeared in the Rhône Valley below. The danger of a wholesale "rural exodus" was forestalled in the 1950s with the canton- and confederation-subsidized construction of an important hydroelectric project on commune territory. For a decade, the dam construction employed a large proportion of the active male population of the commune, leaving the wives and daughters to maintain the farms. Having now removed men from agriculture, the commune faced the problem of losing them entirely upon completion of the dam. At this point, the canton assisted the commune in attracting an electrical appliance firm to establish a small assembly plant on commune territory—explicitly destined to offer employment to local men after completion of the dam. Thus, rather than removing control from the local level, the state—canton and confederation—has helped to introduce new resources into the communal economic structure.

The concept of utilizing all possible local resources—even adding to the stock as necessary—is an economic expression of the political philosophy of communal autonomy and diversity. While the commune is a homogeneous cultural unit, it is integrated organically with other such units and can be differentiated from them along a number of dimensions common to all: historical, geographic and ecological, demographic, political, linguistic, religious, and occupational.

In the commune of Bagnes, this combination of cultural homogeneity and multi-dimensional differentiation is replicated at several levels. The commune maps cognitively into several regions—differentiated by their diversity of interests which arise from ecological, demographic, and occupational differences. The individual villages are further differentiated—along the same dimensions as the regions, as well as according to political and linguistic differences. Differentiation of a still finer grain takes place within the context of the village, with its various voluntary associations, and culminates in an ideology of individual uniqueness.

At each level of differentiation within the commune of Bagnes, there is also a replication of the philosophy behind the inverted state hierarchy: an analytic, problem-solving approach which identifies available resources and leaves their management in the hands of that particular level. Proceeds from the water rights in the dam—a commune-wide resource— are managed by the commune; proceeds from *bourgeoisie*-owned high pasturelands are managed by the village corporations which have local usufructory rights; proceeds from the village dairy are managed by village members of the cooperative; the proceeds of an inheritance are managed by the heir and his or her household; and, ultimately, the benefits of having a particular reputation or expressive nickname are enjoyed and manipulated by the individual.

Since encapsulation means thorough incorporation into a larger system, it also implies an ensuing loss of identity of the smaller subsystem. This is not the case in Switzerland. As one moves *up* the hierarchy of administration, the "whole" becomes more and more elusive and ephemeral. As one moves *down*, however, the "parts" become more distinct and vital. Rather than encapsulation, what one sees is a kind of nesting of subsystems. The image I have in mind is a set of Russian Easter eggs—painted wooden eggs of graduated size, each one nestled within another and simultaneously containing the next smaller. If the set is taken apart, each egg is complete unto itself—a separate integral unit. Put back together, the smallest eggs are most protected and the largest most vulnerable, most in direct contact with the environment. But removal of the largest egg—far from destroying the system—simply reveals the next layer. This system, although an intermediated hierarchy, does not depend for its survival on the largest egg but rather on the successive appearance of each egg. A larger egg does not encapsulate but is simply fitted around the next smaller.

This metaphor aptly describes the Swiss Confederation. There are at least three levels of nesting—the federal, the cantonal, and the communal. Beyond that, in certain cases, there may be even more levels. In a multi-village commune like Bagnes, the commune encases regions which contain villages. The village itself is a nesting of neighborhoods, households, and individuals. Further diversity is achieved within the village through the existence of kinship and voluntary associations which mediate between individual or household and the world outside the village.

The Russian Easter egg aggregate—although it does not reveal the great diversity among subsystems of the Swiss state—does express the common political philosophy which unifies the state: the highest possible degree of integrity and autonomy at each level. The historical primacy of the Swiss commune is also well modeled in the nested eggs, which are crafted from the inside out.

But the most important and interesting attribute of a nested state is the protective buffering it provides at each level of the system. Encapsulation negates identity; nesting promotes it. Encapsulation implies digestion; nesting precludes it. Encapsulation imposes monoculturization on the local community—suburbanization, tourism, or monocropping; nesting encourages the internal variety required for maintaining local autonomy. Recalling the uneasy feudal balance between lord and peasant, one may say that a nested system minimizes subjection and maximizes protection.

In a nested system, therefore, one would expect to see the

highest degree of cultural persistence at the lowest levels. Each
level exists in its own micro-environment. Given some minimum
population size and resource base, the local community should
be able to deal with its micro-environment simply through
regulation rather than through adaptation. The highest level
in the system, however—the federal level—has, in a sense, *more*
environment to deal with and so may be required to make
certain adaptations in order to persist. The federal policy of
neutrality is one such adaptation. It is a particularly clear
example of Romer's Rule, since it effectively denies the existence of an environment.

The structural principle of nesting is not itself sufficiently
explanatory. One must also take into account ecological factors.
Although the smallest "egg" in a nested set should be the most
stable, it may lose some of its structural advantage for survival
by being *too* small. We know, from evolutionary theory, that
survival depends not only on stability but also on some minimum level of variety—a set of alternative responses to meet
changes in the environment. We must, therefore, narrow our initial prediction that cultural persistence is best assured at the
lowest levels of the nested system by adding the proviso that
there is an ecological threshold below which the lowest level
effectively drops out of the nest and can no longer benefit
from the structural protection offered by the system. Thus,
a single-village commune with a small population and a limited
resource base is at the greatest disadvantage. It lacks the
requisite variety to survive in its micro-environment. Such a
commune will tend to be drawn into the environment of the
next higher level—perhaps the nearest city, or, through geographic accident, the canton itself. The dangers of encapsulation and loss of identity are great, but only such a distinct
adaptation will preserve the commune in any form.

The Valaisan commune of Vernamiège (Berthoud 1967) is
an example of this disadvantaged situation. The commune
consists of a single village of about 250 inhabitants. It is located
high up on a steep wall of the valley—too steep either for
agriculture or for ski development. The commune has no other
economic resources such as hydroelectric power. Its single
major resource is human labor which it is exporting to the
nearby cantonal capital of Sion. The commune has become

a bedroom suburb, but even that seems to be only a stopgap adaptation, because the commune continues to depopulate rapidly (Berthoud 1967:70ff).

The Valaisan commune of Trient, on the other hand, has long been a small summer resort area—a stop on the mountaineering route to Mt. Blanc, just over the border in France. Today, it also participates in the exploitation of local water power with the construction of the Emosson dam. The population of Trient has decreased from 130 to 90 over the past fifty years. About one-third of the present population is supported by dam-related employment, and a few of these families have actually moved into the commune from elsewhere. In addition, there has been some population exchange with the nearby city of Martigny—tending to make Trient a bedroom suburb.

Regulation of this type—hydroelectric construction, suburbanization—is too wide-ranging to be stable. When the micro-environment of such a small commune extends from the French tourist resort of Chamonix to the Valaisan market town of Martigny, adaptation will ultimately be forced on the commune, and it will be drawn into a larger orbit.

These examples reveal another aspect of Swiss nesting. Because of the federalist principle of an inverted chain of command which respects local autonomy, a non-viable unit at the lowest level will indeed become "encapsulated"—not into the state but only into the next higher level in the nest. But size-dependence—whether demographic or ecological—may ultimately be superseded by the centralizing pressures which inevitably creep into any modern nation-state. As these pressures move down the chain of command—the nation-state's response to its international environment—they may destroy the concept of minimum viability at the lowest level. In effect, there may *always* be, by definition, a non-viable lowest level in the system, for centralization advocates "efficiency" through the elimination of duplication. A centralized "tree," as I pointed out in the French case, tends to reduce levels of intermediation, and ultimately collapses into a two-level hierarchy with a wide branching ratio—thereby focusing maximum control at the topmost level.

The contemporary Swiss response to centralizing pressures is, in effect, a move toward disintermediation which originates

at the *bottom* levels of the structure. One of the forms this
response has taken recently is the creation of small, localized
agglomerates—regional "federations" of communes with similar
interests which combine forces to meet outside threats to their
existence, in much the same way as their ancestors did in 1291.
No longer able to rely entirely on the protection offered by
the vertical system of nesting, the communes are trying to
broaden their resource base horizontally. These regional alliances are of a specific and limited nature, entailing a partial
and voluntary yielding of commune autonomy: for example,
associations for water purification, waste disposal, touristic
development, and hydroelectric power. They present a chal-
lenge to centralization in the idiom of federalist philosophy:
"keeping one's own house in order," in the words of the Socialist
journalist.

In the commune of Bagnes, environmental regulation has
been greatly facilitated by a large population distributed
among ten major villages, and a varied resource base. Although
Switzerland did not participate in the two World Wars, their
influence was nevertheless felt—in the form of partial mobiliza-
tion for defense and, especially, the cutting off of food imports
from other European countries. During World War I, the
peasants of Bruson, as one informant put it, "tightened their
belts." By the time World War II began, strawberries had been
introduced, the high summer pastures had been consolidated
and improved, and a modern cooperative dairy had replaced
several earlier ones in the village. The peasants, many of them
now peasant-workers, met the national emergency by returning
the strawberry fields to grain.

Shortly after World War II, the narrow-gauge railroad line
was extended from the nearby city of Martigny to reach Le
Châble—the commune seat and entrance to the valley. The
railroad facilitated the rapid touristic development of Verbier
as a ski resort, bringing revenue and employment to the commune as a whole. At the same time, dam construction began
at the head of the valley—further increasing income and work.
With expanded employment opportunities, young people
prepared for non-agricultural careers and older people wel-
comed the opportunity for income to supplement their earnings
from agriculture.

With this expansion of economic alternatives, a certain degree of regional and village specialization began to appear. Participating in a larger system, a particular village could afford to concentrate on its most productive resources. Le Châble—always somewhat specialized as the seat of commune government and the parish and market center—became, in addition, a gateway for tourism. Verbier and the neighboring villages on the north slope became the primary tourist center. Mauvoisin, at the end of the valley and always a modest summer resort, now capitalized on the tourist attraction of the dam, as well as those attractions based on its altitude, mountaineering tradition, and rare fauna and flora. Bruson and Lourtier—because of favorable topography—remained largely agricultural villages. Lourtier also became a center for small game hunting and the gateway to Mauvoisin and the "High Valley of Bagnes," while Bruson, too, became something of a tourist area through the winter exploitation of its fields and pastures. People from villages without solid resource potential found places in other commune activities—in construction, sawmilling, furniture making, hotels and cafés, and other tourism-related enterprises; in the commune administration, which grew increasingly complex with economic development; or even in teaching jobs in the commune schools, which maintained their enrollments because of the braking of the "rural exodus."

Village specialization has been made possible and profitable because of the integration of villages within a larger cultural and political unit—the commune. At the same time, however, specialization has not produced occupational uniformity at the village level. Quite the contrary. Specialization has enabled the continuation of the traditionally mixed economy—necessitated by the micro-variability and marginality of Alpine ecology, and elevated from a principle of behavior to an article of faith.

The traditional mixed economy of Bruson always included agricultural and non-agricultural activities. In the past, the Brusonin was a part-time artisan—in addition to managing his agro-pastoral enterprise. To supplement his agricultural income, he might leave the commune—even the country itself—to work "seasons" as a farm laborer or cowherd in the Savoie, or to find employment in hotels in Marseilles and on the Côte

d'Azur. The agricultural activities of the contemporary Brusonin have been expanded through improved dairy technology
and the addition of market crops, but he still operates a "family
farm" and subscribes to a "family labor commitment" (Franklin
1969:15ff). To this extent, he is still a "peasant"—"someone
who works the land" (a Brusonin's definition). He also retains
the traditional "peasant" characteristic of "someone who does
a little of everything" (a definition from Hérémence)—both
agricultural and non-agricultural. Even those Brusonins who
work full-time at a skilled trade do so, by choice, on an
hourly-wage basis and maintain their agricultural holding
through a family labor force of wife and children supplemented
by their own part-time efforts.

The *principle* of doing "a little of everything" has remained operative, even though there has been some substitution of *content*. Thus, the Brusonin who used to work "seasons"
outside the commune may now be employed as the cheese
maker in the village dairy. The Brusonin who, in the past,
might have earned extra income as the village shoemaker is
now employed on an hourly-wage basis as a carpenter in a
valley firm.

According to Franklin's typology of peasantry, the contemporary Brusonin is neither a "worker-peasant" nor a "part-time
farmer" (1969:220). This distinction is not valid in Bruson, since
every Brusonin with minimal resources of land and labor—
whether or not he is employed outside or runs an additional
business—completely retains both his commitments to and his
managerial functions in his agricultural enterprise. In addition,
most Brusonins who are employed outside their agricultural
enterprises retain a high degree of control of their labor—by
working seasonally, for hourly wages, and by taking the time
off necessary to maintain their farm holdings.

Indeed, some of their employment opportunities are especially and deliberately suited to maintaining this control. The
nearby watch factory and electrical assembly plant, for example, although "industrial" operations, are labor-intensive rather
than capital-intensive. Since production does not depend on
heavy machinery or special power supplies, work can proceed
on a part-time, individually regulated basis and can even be
done at home. Thus, the Brusonin is both "worker-peasant"

and "part-time farmer." His trade is simply another personal resource—along with a hayfield, a cow, a strawberry patch, a jeep, a vineyard, a healthy wife, a willing son-in-law, a widowed mother.

For the Brusonin, the essential quality of "peasantness"—the freedom to manipulate a diversity of resources—has been preserved as a fundamental principle of behavior and tenet of belief. This behavior and belief are enhanced by the special nature of the state in which he participates—the inverted nested hierarchy of autonomous societies in voluntary association with each other. It is paradoxical that, as Bruson has moved into the twentieth century and greatly expanded both its resource base and its autonomy—its "peasantness"—it is ceasing to be a "peasant" village. The economy is still largely a "peasant economy"—based on familistic rather than capitalistic enterprise. But, although the Brusonin is more than ever in "effective control [of his] land" and other resources, he is less than ever "subject to the demands and sanctions of power-holders outside his social stratum." Although more than ever involved in the outside market—through agriculture and through tourism—he is protected from over-dependence on the market by the nested political structure which allows him, more than ever, to broaden his local resource base.

It is remarkable that both kinds of political structure—the encapsulating bureaucratic "tree" and the inverted nesting—ultimately transform the peasantry. While an encapsulated peasantry rapidly becomes a non-peasantry, the transformation of a nested peasantry is conservative, gradual, and subtle. In the Swiss case, because of the inverted chain of control, this transformation also tends to be self-regulatory and more responsive to changes in the environment. Viewing such a system, one is more impressed with the force of cultural stability than with manifestations of culture change.

21. Continuity and Change

Were Brusonins *ever* peasants—according to standard definitions of that term?

In the Middle Ages, Swiss rural peoples were only minimally subjected to feudal control. The Swiss state grew from the bottom up, by voluntary and gradual accretion, and has preserved its primary function of guaranteeing the autonomy of its member parts. The Great and Little Traditions model is therefore not applicable here—not only because of this unique history of state development, but also because of the relative absence of urban concentrations of high culture and elite groups.

Urbanization of the Swiss plateau, although not negligible even before the industrial era, has never been intense. Certainly, industrial development involved—as it did everywhere—the formation of sizeable urban concentrations. But the conditions peculiar to Swiss industry have prevented the creation of immense cities, taking over all the productive efforts of the nation: the absence of large complexes of heavy industry; the possibility of dispersing the major manufacturing industries (textiles, timepieces); and a specialized but not large labor force. (Bergier 1968:22)

Today, the largest city in Switzerland, Zürich, has a population of just over 400,000—about the size of Omaha, Nebraska. Only about 20 percent of the total population of some six million live in communities of over 100,000. Another 25 percent live in communities of over 10,000. The remaining 45 percent live in communities smaller than Martigny (about 10,000). It is not surprising, then, that the "little communities" have contributed many painters, writers, and thinkers to the Swiss national heritage—the "Great Tradition." Bagnes, for example, is known for its exportation of teachers, clerics, and missionaries; the commune has also produced writers and poets (Louis Courthion, fl.1900; Alfred Besse-Deslarzes, fl.1880), an important deputy to the federal parliament (Maurice Troillet, 1880-1961), and a peasant-mountain guide who first suggested the modern theory of glaciology (Jean-Pierre Perraudin, fl. 1820).

Neither feudalism, nor the state, nor urban elites have been effective in subjugating the Swiss peasantry—in pressing demands on it to increase their "funds of power." The Swiss peasant has always been in "effective control of his land," and in fact, that land has been the primary "power-holder" in his society. The same topography and climate that makes Alpine valleys easy to defend also makes them harsh masters of agriculture. The successful struggle to regulate this difficult environment has therefore produced what appears to be the very antithesis of "peasantry": a "republic" of Bagnes, consisting of free, land-owning individuals.

The strategy for survival in this Alpine ecology has been built on the tactics of independent owners manipulating a variety of resources within the context of a local community of kinsmen, neighbors, and associates. As new resources are added to the stock, and as individuals move more freely in and out, articulation between the village and the outside world grows—increasing engagement of Brusonins in the part-whole relationship. These new commitments outside the village—the direct result of successful regulation of the environment—have produced a modern version of the part-society and of the peasant dilemma. The adaptive *success* of Bruson now presents a greater threat to cultural survival than its history of natural catastrophes ever posed.

The problem faced by the individual Brusonin may be

sketched broadly. Increased income, expanded employment opportunities, greater demands for physical comfort, and higher aspirations for his children—each conceals an intrinsic threat to his self-image as a free agent. The traditional ideology of "peasant wisdom"—the wisdom to remain free of outside control by owning and managing a variety of resources, and free of debt by running a self-supporting household—is being undermined by the increasing presence of capitalism in the commune. Capitalistic tourism urges that land and labor be treated as commodities. The Brusonin has always known how to sell his *labor*—although on a very controlled basis; now he is encouraged to sell his *land*—or at least to invest in the construction of rental properties.

The Brusonin's problem is complicated by the evolution of his village community—the context in which he is a free individual. The economic development of the commune has removed a number of village functions to higher levels of organization. Half a century ago, the village *quartiers* were still functioning mutual-aid units. Each had its fountain—whose major functions have been replaced by indoor water provided by the commune. Each had access to a communal oven in which bread was baked four times a year, but this family bread-baking was superseded by individual artisanry—the village baker. Since his death in 1968, bread is supplied to the village by bakers in Le Châble and sold, at prices controlled by the Confederation, in the two village shops.

Another important village function—the *chef de travail*—has been gradually preempted by both commune and canton. The chef de travail was elected in the traditional annual village meeting in December, the *Assemblée de St.-Martin*, and was in charge of organizing corvées for village public works—road work, garbage collection and disposal, snow clearance. Though the elections are still held in the traditional manner, the present chef de travail has little real work to do: the canton employs another villager in road work and snow clearance; the commune collects the garbage. Even the traditional village fire squad is now paid by the Confederation.

The services of part-time village artisans have been displaced to Le Châble and sometimes as far away as Martigny. Those villagers who *have* maintained their trades often work at them on a full-time basis in business firms elsewhere in the commune. When the commune provided Bruson with a community freezer in 1963, several other traditional crafts began to disappear— butchering, and meat preservation through salting and drying.

As it preempts village functions, commune intervention broadens the network of social relations. With the atrophy of the quartiers and their consolidation from the outside into a single village unit, interpersonal relations begin to move outside quartier boundaries and to be extended to the village as a whole. While the local quartier was once a close-knit group of cooperating neighbors linked in the easy reciprocity of long-standing relations of mutual-aid, the larger village unit is now cross-cut by ties of instrumental friendship and a service-payment approach to reciprocity. This form of reciprocity is more appropriate to such a group and is modeled, in part at least, on the kind of "reciprocity" perceived in the outside, capitalistic, monetized world.

Simplification of village functions and reduction in self-sufficiency have been accompanied by complexification of the occupational structure and a corresponding increase in the self-sufficiency of the *ménage*. However, the Brusonin who turns to the outside economy is less secure in his village anchor today than a generation ago. The village, in turn is less confident of maintaining his continuing presence and thereby enjoying a portion of the fruits of his outside labor.

From the point of view of a peasantry, the ideal part-society configuration enables those who can to "plug in" to the larger society—by selling their labor or their produce—and those who cannot to be provided for in the local community. The ideal "plug" is optative and temporary—allowing free movement back and forth between the two sectors, so that material goods, services, and knowledge can flow back into the village. This two-way flow must be maintained, so "plugging in" must not be attractive enough to become irreversible. On the other hand, "plugging in" must not be made too difficult—as by constraints of distance or accessibility. If either of these constraints becomes too great, they can have an engulfing and committing effect on the individual, thereby removing him permanently from the village and arresting the beneficial flow.

The nested Swiss political system facilitates this kind of

part-whole relationship. The Swiss peasant dilemma is to balance not demands, but attractions. Every occasion of "plugging in" is potentially beneficial and, by the same token, threatening to the village community. Put another way, every improvement in the *conditions* of life has its cost in the *quality* of life. In Bruson, the quality of life depends on individual freedom within a vital community. Traditionally, vitality has meant economic self-sufficiency—a solidary community composed of self-provisioning and debt-free ménages, and expressed in the collective self-image of Bruson as a hospitable village. Just as the individual represents his ménage when he offers wine in the café, the *procureur* represents the village when she "receives the priest" with the hospitality for which the village is known. In each case, the wine and food are the products of an ongoing peasant economy—of one's own land, worked by one's own family.

The distance between the traditional quartier relationships of mutual aid and the modern cases of cash payment for professional services represents the increasing distinction between things and persons discussed by Mauss. He described an evolutionary continuum which begins

> in these 'early' societies, [where] social phenomena are not discrete; each phenomenon contains all the threads of which the social fabric is composed. In these *total* social phenomena, as we propose to call them, all kinds of institutions find simultaneous expression: religious, legal, moral, and economic. (Mauss 1967:1)

At this end of the continuum, one finds "total prestations"— exchanges between groups, rather than individuals, of

> not exclusively goods and wealth, real and personal property, and things of economic value. They exchange rather courtesies, entertainments, ritual, military assistance, women, children, dances, and feasts. (Mauss 1967:3)

From total prestation, one moves, through interpersonal gift exchange, to

> pure individual contract, the money market, sale proper, fixed price, and weighed and coined money. (Mauss 1967:45)

For a Brusonin today, contract exchange represents the outside, the "plug-in" world, in which he has difficulty maintaining his self-image as a free individual. Simultaneously, the increasing disintermediation and simplification of the village tends to leave him, not free, but free-floating. In response to these pressures, Brusonins have constructed—out of traditional materials—a system of exchange relationships expressing "simultaneous intimacy [the "one family" village unit] and distance [the independent individual]" (Mauss 1967:18).

The theme of the gift, of freedom and obligation in the gift, of generosity and self-interest in giving, reappear in our own society like the resurrection of a dominant motif long forgotten ... Societies have progressed in the measure in which they, their sub-groups and their members, have been able to stabilize their contracts and to give, receive and repay. (Mauss 1967:80)

In Bruson this stabilization of contracts takes place in the context of the "one family" that is the entire village. The village-wide kinship network—based on an assumption of common descent from a group of founding *ancêtres*—simultaneously generates a universal network of instrumental relations and suppresses purely affective relations. "Best friends" are adventitious to the village social system and persist, in very attenuated form, only in the private sphere. The easy friendships of the traditional quartier, extended to the village as a whole, have become formalized and circumscribed by ritual and prescription. The "rules" of interaction at the village level assure maintenance of the "one family" fiction by prescribing an attitude of free mutual aid such as exists within the ménage and the converging family. Proper observance of these "rules" corrects any momentary imbalance between individuals—an imbalance which would not, by definition, be perceived within the family itself, and which thus threatens to reveal the "one family" as a fiction.

Clearly, these dramatizations of reciprocity are "total social phenomena" which blur the distinction between people and objects. Should an object threaten to emerge as the real content of an exchange event, the situation is quickly returned to the safety of the "one family" context through the ménage idiom

of commensality. Thus, cash payment for a professional service
is immediately followed by the "gift" of ménage hospitality:
"Allons boire un verre." Even services which neither require
nor permit "payment" in the monetary currency of the outside
world are "paid" for in "one family" currency—to avoid any
taint of debt or even insufficiency: *"Je te paye un verre."* The
currency is that of a peasant economy. The exchange is between
free, self-provisioning individuals who own their property and
exploit it with family labor.

Since women still move in a very traditional culture, they
provide a model for this behavior and a counterweight to the
encroachment of the outside world which makes it necessary.
Their public appearances are generally confined to the economic base of the ménage: stable, barn, fields, and vineyards. Yet,
though women are the full-time agriculturalists of the ménage,
no woman gives her occupation as "agriculturalist." The
universal label of "housewife"—*ménagère*—reveals the intrinsic
and traditional bond between social and economic threads in
the societal fabric. Since women are restricted to ménage
territory, they continue to engage in the easy relationships of
the quartier—even though it has lost its status as a well-defined
social unit. Men, on the other hand, are more removed from
their traditional occupations and in daily contact with the
outside world, so their interactions must be dramatized and
formalized.

The village's perception of its evolution is also revealed in
the treatment of voluntary associations. The *consortage*—the
traditional *alpage* association—is referred to as a "community"—not the modern dairy or fruit and vegetable cooperatives.
The consortage is a "necessary evil," but the other cooperative
associations are profitable. The consortage belongs to the traditional past; the others, to the capitalistic present. Membership
in the consortage is membership in the "one family" inherited
along with one's name, *bourgeoisie*, political affiliation, and
property base and attesting to the traditional peasant vocation
of the community. Adherence to the other associations, however, is a matter for individual, self-interested choice. Although
the presumptive reason for the existence of the consortage is
economic, the increasing cost of its persistence requires a
non-economic explanation. The consortage—an unprofitable

economic enterprise—is more like those associations I have described as being diffuse in purpose and not directly tied to the economic welfare of the village. The image Brusonins hold of the consortage as a "community" is consonant with this diffuseness of purpose.

The consortage, the singing society, the political *cercle*—all these are total social phenomena which identify the villager as a Brusonin. They are laced with kinship bonds, bolstered by history, and presented to the outside world as specifically Brusonin manifestations. On the internal stage of social relations, villagers cooperate in the "one family" drama—playing their roles as independent peasant producers only incidentally and voluntarily articulated with the larger capitalist economy. The response to outside encroachment on the village has been the reinforcement of an adaptive anachronism—*peasantry*:

> The existence of a peasantry thus involves not merely a relation between peasant and nonpeasant, but a type of adaptation, a combination of attitudes and activities designed to sustain the cultivator in his effort to maintain himself and his kind within a social order which threatens that maintenance. (Wolf 1966b:17)

In this fundamental sense of "peasantry"—as "a type of adaptation"—Bruson is today more of a peasant village than ever before. It is a part-society whose distinctive part-culture has been guaranteed by the larger political system and maintained internally through a variety of economic, social structural, and ideological mechanisms. The difficult ecological situation has produced "a combination of attitudes and activities" which Brusonins call "peasant wisdom." Most clearly expressed in the management of tension between individual and community, peasant wisdom continues to serve the village well as it faces the modern social order.

I have examined "peasantries" of the past as adaptive systems. I have followed some of them through their increasingly unsuccessful attempts at regulation of the environment to their ultimate transformation into "non-peasantries." Applying the same diagnostic models to Bruson, one finds oneself studying not culture change but cultural continuity. I have generalized the meaning of part-society from exploitation to functional dependence; of part-culture to solidary distinctiveness; of the part-whole relationship to a controlled but vital dialogue. It is taking a small but significant step beyond earlier understandings of peasantry to learn to regard "peasantry" not as a culture type, but as an adaptive system.

Bibliography

Andan, Odile
  1965 *Bruson, Essai de Modernisation d'un Village de Montagne en Valais*. Lausanne: Imprimerie Louis Couchoud S.A.

Anderson, Robert T., and Gallatin Anderson
  1962 The Replicate Social Structure. *Southwestern Journal of Anthropology* 18:365-370.

Bailey, F. G., ed.
  1969 *Stratagems and Spoils: A Social Anthropology of Politics*. New York: Schocken Books.
  1971 *Gifts and Poison. The Politics of Reputation*. New York: Schocken Books.

Bérard, Clement
  1963 *Bataille pour l'Eau*. Martigny: Pillet.

Bergier, Jean-François
  1968 *Problèmes de l'Histoire Economique de la Suisse*. Bern: Francke Editions.

Berthoud, Gérald
  1967 *Changements Economiques et Sociaux de la Montagne. Vernamiège en Valais*. Berne: Editions Francke.

Bjerrome, Gunnar
  1957 *Le Patois de Bagnes (Valais)*. Stockholm: Almquist and Wiksell.

Bloch, Marc
  1966 *French Rural History. An Essay on its Basic Characteristics*. (1931) Berkeley and Los Angeles: University of California Press.

Boltanski, Luc
  1966 *Le Bonheur Suisse*. Paris: Les Editions de Minuit.

Bonjour, Edgar, H. S. Offler, and G. R. Potter
  1952   *A Short History of Switzerland*. Oxford: Clarendon Press.
Bozon, Pierre
  1970   Le Pays des Villards en Maurienne. *Editions des Cahiers de l'Alpe, Collection "Histoire Regionale."* Grenoble: Allier.
Burns, Robert K., Jr.
  1959   Saint Véran, France's Highest Village. *National Geographic Magazine*, Vol. CXV no. 4 (April).
  1963   The Circum-Alpine Culture Area: A Preliminary View. *Anthropological Quarterly* 36:3.
Chappaz, Maurice
  1965   *Portrait des Valaisans en Légende et en Verité*. Lausanne: Cahiers de la Renaissance Vaudoise.
Courthion, Louis
  1893   Esquisse Historique de la Vallée et de la Commune de Bagnes-en-Valais. *Revue Historique Vaudoise*.
  1896   *Les Veillées des Mayens*. Genève: A. Jullien.
  1972   *Le Peuple du Valais*. (1903) Lausanne: Bibliothèque Romande.
  1907   *Bagnes-Entremont-Ferrex*. Genève: A. Jullien.
  1916   La Vie Communale en Valais. *Wissen und Leben*, October.
Deutsch, Karl, and Hermann Weilenmann
  1965   The Swiss City Canton: A Political Invention. *Comparative Studies in Society and History* 7.
F. A. O.
  1959   Situation Economique et Sociale de la Population Montagnarde en Suisse. Bern: Département Fédéral de l'Economie, Division de l'Agriculture.
Fallers, L. A.
  1961   Are African Cultivators to be Called "Peasants"? *Current Anthropology*, vol. II (April). *Reprinted in*: Potter et al. 1967.
Franklin, S. H.
  1969   *The European Peasantry. The Final Phase*. London: Methuen.
Friedl, John
  1974   *Kippel: A Changing Village in the Alps*. New York: Holt, Rinehart and Winston.
Gabert, Pierre, and Paul Guichonnet
  1965   *Les Alpes et Les Etats Alpins*. Paris: Presses Universitaires de France.
Geertz, Clifford
  1959   Form and Variation in Balinese Village Structure. *American Anthropologist* 61, 6. *Reprinted in*: Potter et al. 1967.
Gossop, Elizabeth J.
  1964   Recent Population Trends and Economic Changes in Two Alpine Valleys. The Val de Bagnes (Valais, Switzerland) and Valpelline (Aosta, Italy). Unpublished thesis. Cambridge University, Cambridge.

Gsell, Daniela
  n.d. *Ernahrungs- und Gesundheitszustand in Bruson-Bagnes (Wallis).*
        Zurich: Eidegenossischen Ernahrungskommission/Subkommission
        für die Bergbevolkerung.
Gutersohn, Heinrich
  1961 *Géographie der Schweiz.* t.II,1: Wallis, Tessin, Graubunden. Bern:
        Kümmerly and Frey.
Jusserand, J. J.
  1961 *English Wayfaring Life in the Middle Ages.* (1889) Lucy Toulmin
        Smith, transl. New York: Barnes and Noble.
Kroeber, Alfred L.
  1948 *Anthropology.* New York: Harcourt, Brace and World.
Kümmerly and Frey
  1962 *Switzerland.* Bern: Kümmerly and Frey.
Lobsiger, Georges
  1966 Quelques Aspects de la Population Suisse. "Globe," No. 106 (Mé-
        moires). *Société de Géographie de Genève.* Genève: Athenée.
Loup, Jean
  1965 *Pasteurs et Agriculteurs Valaisans. Contribution à l'étude des
        problèmes montagnards.* Grenoble: Imprimerie Allier.
Mauss, Marcel
  1967 *The Gift. (Essai sur le Don. 1925)* Ian Cunnison, transl. New York:
        W. W. Norton.
Mendras, Henri
  1970 *The Vanishing Peasant: Innovation and Change in French Agri-
        culture.* Cambridge: M.I.T. Press.
Mintz, Sidney W., and Eric R. Wolf
  1950 An Analysis of Ritual Co-Parenthood (Compadrazgo). *Southwes-
        tern Journal of Anthropology* VI. *Reprinted in:* Potter et al. 1967.
Moore, Barrington, Jr.
  1966 *Social Origins of Dictatorship and Democracy. Lord and Peasant
        in the Making of the Modern World.* Boston: Beacon Press.
Mutton, Alice F. A.
  1961 *Central Europe. A Regional and Human Geography.* New York:
        John Wiley and Sons, Inc.
Naroll, Raoul
  1964 Some Problems for Research in Switzerland. *In:* Symposium on
        Community Studies in Anthropology. V. E. Garfield and E. Friedl,
        eds. Seattle: University of Washington Press.
Netting, Robert McC.
  1972 Of Men and Meadows: Strategies of Alpine Land Use. *Anthro-
        pological Quarterly* 45, 3 (July).
Perraudin, Francis
  n.d. *Mauvoisin dans le Haut Val de Bagnes.*
Potter, Jack M., May N. Diaz, George M. Foster
  1967 *Peasant Society. A Reader.* Boston: Little, Brown and Co.

Ramuz, C. F.
  1968   *Farinet, ou La Fausse Monnaie*. Bienne: Collection "L'Eventail,"
         Marguerat.
Redfield, Robert
  1956   *The Little Community, and Peasant Society and Culture*. Chicago:
         University of Chicago Press.
Redfield, Robert, and Milton B. Singer
  1954   The Cultural Role of Cities. *Economic Development and Cultural
         Change* 3.
Reiter, Rayna R.
  1972   Modernization in the South of France: The Village and Beyond.
         Anthropological Quarterly 45, 1 (January).
Rosset, Lucien
  1973   Zones vertes: les députés voient rouge. *Le Peuple Valaisan*, July
         6.
Rougemont, Denis de
  1970   *La Suisse, ou l'Histoire d'un Peuple Heureux*. Lausanne: Le Livre
         du Mois (1965).
Sauser-Hall, Georges
  1965   *Guide Politique Suisse*. Lausanne: Payot.
Sauter, Marc-R.
  1950   Préhistoire du Valais. Des Origines aux Temps Mérovingiens. *Vallé-
         sia* V.
Schneider, David M.
  1968   *American Kinship: A Cultural Account*. New Jersey: Prentice-Hall.
Service, Elman R.
  1962   *Primitive Social Organization*. New York: Random House.
Siegfried, André
  1956   *La Suisse, Démocratie Témoin*. Neuchatel: Baconniere. 3rd ed.
         (1948).
Skinner, G. William
  1964   Marketing and Social Structure in Rural China, Part I. *Journal
         of Asian Studies*, Vol. XXIV no. 1 (November). *Reprinted in*: Potter
         et al. 1967.
Suter, Karl
  1944   L'Economie Alpestre au Val de Bagnes. Essai Géographique. *Bulle-
         tin de la Murithienne*, fascicule LXI, 1943-1944.
Valarché, Jean
  1960   L'Organisation Sociale Rurale du Valais et son Evolution. *Revue
         Suisse d'Economie et de Statistique*.
Vallat, Jean
  1966   Développement Rural à Bruson. Village de Montagne dans le
         Canton du Valais. Paris: Organisation de Cooperation et de Déve-
         loppement Economiques.
Weinberg, Daniela
  1972   Cutting the Pie in the Swiss Alps. *Anthropological Quarterly*, 45,
         3 (July).

Weinberg, Daniela, and Gerald M. Weinberg
  1972 Using a Computer in the Field: Kinship Information. *Social Science Information*, 11,6 (December).
Windisch, Uli
  1971 Société Rurale, Développement Touristique, Pouvoir Politique et Conscience de Classe. *Cahiers Vilfredo Pareto* 25:121-183. Genève: Librairie Droz.
Wolf, Eric R.
  1957 Closed Corporate Peasant Communities in Mesoamerica and Central Java. *Southwestern Journal of Anthropology* 13, 1. *Reprinted in*: Potter et al. 1967.
  1966a Kinship, Friendship, and Patron-Client Relations in Complex Societies. *In*: Michael Banton, ed., The Social Anthropology of Complex Societies, *ASA Monographs* No. 4. London: Tavistock.
  1966b *Peasants*. Englewood Cliffs, New Jersey: Prentice-Hall.
Wylie, Laurence
  1963 Demographic Change in Roussillon. *In*: Julian Pitt-Rivers, ed., *Mediterranean Countrymen*. Paris: Mouton.

Index

209

Church, 161, 164
Citizenship. See *Bourgeoisie*
Classe, 119, 142; membership, 142
Climate, 12
Cognatic descent group, 93
Collective personality, 102; as village identity, 101; of group, 135
Colpied, 158, 184
Commandant, 69
Commerce, women in, 47-54
Commercial relationship, 73
Commissaire, 71
Committee, 133
Common descent group, 94
Common Market, 23
Common residence, 155
Communal autonomy, 173
Commune, 155, 171, 177, 191; *bourgeois*, 173; *d'assistance*, 173; definition of, 9; *ecclésiastique*, 173; of Bagnes, 10, 172; *scolaire*, 173
Communities, ix
Community closure, 162
Community-study method, ix
Compadrazgo, 162
Competition, 150, 151
Computer, 112
Concept, part-society, 178
Conceptual village, 156
Confederation, 171, 181, 196; purpose of, 5
Conseil communal, 173, 177
Conseil d'Etat, 182; des Etats, 172; Général, 173; National, 172
Conseillers, 69
Consensus, 178
Conservative Party *cercle*, 131
Conservatives, 144, 174
Consortage, 21, 183, 200
Consortages, 105, 133; history of, 25
Constituent Assembly, 168
Constitution, 172
Continuity and change, 194-202
Converging family, 78, 85, 149f., 199; visits between, 62-63; work groups, 109
Copain, 119
Co-parents, 162
Core families, 91, 158
Corvées, 196
Cosmological system, 88, 93
Cost of living, 23
Courthion, Louis, 158, 160, 183, 195
Covert payment, 50
Cravegna, xii
Creditor, 40-41
Criteria for leadership, 133-134
Cultivated fields, 16

Cultural deviance, 170
Cultural distinctiveness, 164
Cultural heterogeneity, 172
Cultural homogeneity, 186
Cultural pluralism, 170-183 *passim*
Cultural stability, 193
Cultural survival, 195
Culture change, 193; model of, x; vs. culture continuity, 201
Currency, commercial, 40, 41-42
Currency, ideal, 40

Dairy. See *Laiterie*
Dairying, 20-21; cheese production, 23; division of labor in, 21
Debt, 39, 40, 45, 48, 96, 143, 149; village's, 66
Debtor, 40-41
Democrate-Chrétien-Social, 131
Demographic analysis, 142
Demography, 31, 88f.
Depopulation, 158
Dîner, 74
Discrimination, 99
Division of labor, 22
Domestic group. See *Ménage*
Drink, 45; as ideal currency, 40
Drinking, 38
Dwellings, 17; inheritance of, 105

Early history, 15, 19
Eccentricity: antisocial, 123; limits of, 122-123
Ecology, Alpine, 191, 195
Economic associations, 183
Economic cooperation, 25
Economic cooperative, 132, 136
Economic corporations, 183; commune as, 173
Economic events, 38-39
Economic exchanges, 58
Economic structure, 17
Economy, 20-27; dependence vs. independence, 24; shift in, 23; subsistence, 45
Education, 23
Egalitarian ideology, 151
Egocentric unit, 93
Elite groups, 194
Emigration, 116; forced, 19
Emosson Dam, 189
Encapsulation, 184, 186; vs. nesting, 187
Enemies, 79
Enfranchisement of women, x
Environmental protection, 181
Enviormental regulation, 190
Epicerie, 51, 52
Ethnocentric present, x